The Visual Dictionary of Fashion Design

An AVA Book
Published by AVA Publishing SA
Rue des Fontenailles 16
Case Postale
1000 Lausanne 6
Switzerland
Tel: +41 786 005 109
Email: enquiries@avabooks.ch

Distributed by Thames & Hudson (ex-North America)
181a High Holborn
London WC1V 7QX
United Kingdom
Tel: +44 20 7845 5000
Fax: +44 20 7845 5055
Email: sales@thameshudson.co.uk
www.thamesandhudson.com

Distributed in the USA & Canada by
Watson-Guptill Publications
770 Broadway
New York, New York 10003
USA
Fax: +1 646 654 5487
Email: info@watsonguptill.com
www.watsonguptill.com

English Language Support Office
AVA Publishing (UK) Ltd.
Tel: +44 1903 204 455
Email: enquiries@avabooks.co.uk

ISBN 978-2-940373-61-1 and 2-940373-61-2

10 9 8 7 6 5 4 3 2 1

Design by Gavin Ambrose
www.gavinambrose.co.uk

Production by AVA Book Production
Pte. Ltd., Singapore
Tel: +65 6334 8173
Fax: +65 6259 9830
Email: production@avabooks.com.sg

The Visual Dictionary of Fashion Design

This book is an easy-to-use reference to the key terms employed in fashion design. Each entry comprises a brief textual definition along with an illustration or visual example of the point under discussion. Supplementary contextual information is also included.

Key areas addressed in this book are those terms commonly used in reference to fashion design, its history and production.

S Stole   226

A band of cloth or a shawl worn around the shoulders and left to fall down the body front such as a fox-fur stole or mink. Deriving from the Latin *stola* meaning garment or equipment, it is also a Christian vestment, made from an embroidered band of silk. Pictured is a 1962 photograph by John French showing a silk evening dress trimmed with fur and matching stole designed by Nina Ricci worn by Anne Larsen.

see Draping 94

S Stripe   227

A straight band or line differing in colour to that on either side of it. Stripes that may be printed, sewn, woven or knitted into the fabric. Vertical stripes can help give an elongated appearance, making people look thinner, while horizontal stripes often tend to accentuate the girth of the wearer.

Entries are presented in alphabetical order to provide an easy reference system.

T Top Hat   246

A tall, flat-crowned, broad-brimmed hat first made by John Hetherington in 1797 and worn by men throughout the 19th century for business and social events. Made from stiffened beaver fur felt or silk, the top hat or 'topper' declined in popularity towards the end of the century, but was retained for formal occasions by the upper class and continues to be used for formal wear such as with a morning suit and evening dress.

see Hats 128

T Topstitch   247

A sewing technique used for item edges that gives a crisp edge and helps facings (fabric sewn over the base fabric) stay in place. Topstitching may use a thread that matches the colour of the fabric or use a contrasting colour, such as the orange thread used for denim jeans and jackets. Topstitch may also be used to form decorative designs in different coloured thread. Pictured is a piece of leather that has been topstitched for decorative purposes.

see Stitches 225

Footwear extending to the ankle, worn to protect the feet and made in a range of styles and materials such as leather, plastic, rubber or canvas. The main elements of a shoe are the insole, the interior bottom of the shoe that sits under the foot; the outsole, the part in direct contact with the ground; the heel (the bottom rear part of a shoe); the vamp or upper that covers the foot and helps hold the shoe on to it; and the tongue, a flap that is part of the upper and sits underneath the shoelaces.

* The plastic or metal cladding on the end of shoelaces that prevents the twine from unravelling.

see Boots 49, Shoe Types 219

Shoes are available in a range of different styles that readily reflect the changing nature of fashion.

Espadrilles — A wedge shoe with a sole/heel of braided rope.

Flip-flop — A flat sandal with one or two straps between the big and second toes. Also called thongs.

Slide — An open-toed and open-back sandal with one band across the toes.

Ballet flat — A flat shoe with a round toe and thin sole.

Mary Jane — A shoe with a strap across the vamp.

Ankle strap — A sandal with an adjustable strap attached to the back of the shoe passing across the ankle.

Court — A closed-toe shoe with a medium to high heel with pointed or rounded toe.

Clog — A shoe with a wooden, often platform sole. Also called mules.

Stiletto — A court shoe with a high, spiked heel.

Each page or spread contains a single entry and, where appropriate, a printer's hand symbol ☞ provides page references to other related and relevant entries.

A timeline of fashion design helps to provide historical context for selected key moments in the discipline's development.

Welcome to *The Visual Dictionary of Fashion Design*, a book that provides textual definitions and visual explanations for common terms found in the key areas of fashion design and pertinent entries from the wider world of fashion.

This volume aims to provide a clear understanding of the many terms that are often misused or confused, such as *baby doll* and *basque*, or the difference between *calico* and *damask*. As you might expect, *The Visual Dictionary of Fashion Design* provides visual explanations, many of which show garments made by leading designers, to illustrate the correct usage of different concepts, such as *shoes*, *hemlines* and *cuffs*.

Andrei Nekrassov

Tomasz Slowinski

Mossista Pambudi

Tomasz Slowinski

Far left: A modern interpretation of millinery, in the form of a bandana by Rudy Chandra.

Left: Detail of a menswear jacket.

Fashion communicates through a range of visual devices including *montages*, *collages*, *metaphors*, *rhetoric* and *juxtapositions*, all of which, and more, are explained and illustrated in this book.

A clear understanding of the key terms used in fashion design will help you to better articulate and formalise your ideas and will ensure greater accuracy in the transfer of those ideas to others.

Right: An illustration showing horizontal and vertical stripes, which can sometimes affect the perceived size of a dress or garment.

Facing page, far left: A tailor's dummy.

Facing page, left: Various button styles.

Right: A sketch of a design for a men's casual clothing ensemble.

Far right: An illustration of a woman being measured for a dress fitting. During a dress fitting temporary basting or tacking stitches are made to hold seams until they can be permanently sewn.

Facing page: A range of different shirt collar types.

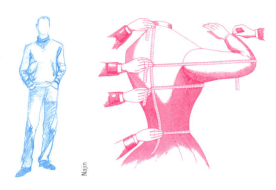

Najin

Fashion design is a discipline that continues to evolve. The timeline at the end of this book (page 274–285) shows how changes in style, zeitgeist and fabrics have dramatically affected the development and evolution of fashion in the past and how, with technological advancements, they continue to do so, as the ever-changing taste and preference of society gives rise to numerous schools of thought about how clothes should look and perform. In the 20th century, for example, the rise of postmodernism saw the development of seemingly 'unfinished' garments with seams on the outside as a rejection of the traditional clothing forms we are more familiar with. However, other designers are also often keen to return to and rediscover more graceful forms and embrace more elaborate and softer visual concepts.

9

Barrymore

Wing

Ascot

Tab

Windsor

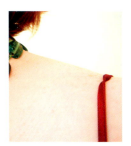

Natalia Mikhaylova

Far left: Detail of a spaghetti strap on a top or dress.

Left: A classic 'little black dress' – an essential for every woman's closet.

Below: An illustration depicting a range of Victorian millinery.

Above left: *Strawberry Thief Chintz,* a floral fabric designed by William Morris in 1883.

Above right: An illustration of a bias-cut dress.

Fashion professionals can draw inspiration from innumerable sources, such as their urban environment, their passions, or by cross-referencing elements of contemporary life with those of bygone days and delving back into the rich tradition of the arts as a means of visual stimulation. Inspiration is key to the generation of exciting design ideas. It is with this in mind that we hope this book will also serve as a source of ideas to inspire your creativity.

Contents

The Dictionary

ACCESSORIES

Zoe Irvin

Extraneous items that complement a whole outfit, such as hats, bags, jewellery and cuff links. Accessories can add sparkle and interesting detail to a plain outfit and can make the same outfit appear very different on separate occasions.

☞ see Garment 118, Hats 128, Jewellery 142, Tie 243

Paid communication that links a sponsor to a message. Advertisements can be presented to the public in a variety of media including television, magazines, radio, billboards, mailers and the Internet (for which advertising revenue forms the business backbone). As the collections of different designers compete for the reader's attention in the turn of a page, fashion industry advertising in magazines has seen the development of highly innovative concepts, finished to the highest printing standards. Pictured is a print advertisement created by 3 Deep Design for Australian designer Toni Maticevski.

☞ see Magazine 157

Nicolas Raymond

Wool from the Andean mammal, the alpaca, is spun into a fine yarn and often woven with other natural fibres, such as protein fibres. Alpaca wool produces a luxurious fabric available in a range of natural colours and is used for sweaters, wraps, hats and gloves, and other woollens. Alpaca wool is hypo-allergenic and naturally flame retardant. Once reserved for Inca royalty, it is warmer than cashmere, lightweight and extremely soft. Pictured is an alpaca near the Inca city of Machu Picchu in Peru. Alpaca wool is available in various degrees of fineness:

Royal Alpaca = 19 microns
Baby Alpaca = 22.5 microns
Super Fine Alpaca = 25.5 microns
Coarse Alpaca = 32 microns.

☞ see Fabric 107, Hats 128, Protein Fabrics 199

Both masculine and feminine traits blended into one unified style, or a lack of specific gender identification. The look includes formal tailoring, military jackets, waistcoats and over-sized dress shirts, enhanced by the use of fabrics such as tweed and velvet. Designers working within the androgynous revolution include Giorgio Armani, Pierre Cardin and Helmut Lang. Androgyny is a fashion statement challenging concepts about gender rather than sexuality.

ChipPix

☞ see Concept 74, Tailoring 232

A dress style that reflects the cyber subculture based on Japanese Anime cartoons. Anime (a contraction of 'animation') features characters that are often androgynous in appearance with large eyes, brightly coloured streaked hair and punk-style clothing.

zmajdoo

☞ see Androgynous 21, Cyber 84

mypokcik

From the French, *appliquer*, meaning to apply.
This is a method of decorating garments (although not
restricted solely to clothes), whereby pieces of fabric
or other materials, such as beads and sequins, are sewn
on to a foundation fabric. Appliqués can be combined
with different types of needlework to create
luxurious designs.

☞ see Fabric 107, Garment 118

Creating the visual concept, look and feel for the presentation of a clothing collection, fashion show or photo shoot, whether for an advertising campaign or magazine spread. Art direction involves the creation of a mood or narrative through which a viewer receives and interprets the subject matter presented to them. Pictured are spreads created by 3 Deep Design for *Poster* magazine. The art direction establishes various simple, but poignant moments in the day of a man, which lead the viewer to assume certain things about his character.

☞ see Advertising 19, Magazine 157

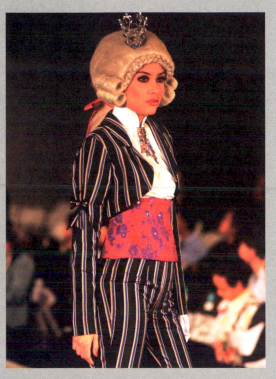

Mosista Pamburi

Creative experimentation that fragments or rejects the norm.
Avant-garde means being at the leading edge or vanguard and is
applied to the most advanced, progressive and experimental
fashions of the moment and prevents the industry from
stagnating. Avant-garde fashions that are exhibited on the
catwalk are often toned down to create more wearable
garments that can be sold in retail stores.

☞ see Garment 118

Zoe Irvin

A short nightgown or négligée (and even daywear when worn over leggings or skinny jeans). A baby doll nightdress is designed to be provocative and is often made from a transparent fabric, such as chiffon and decorated with lace, bows, appliqués and other adornments. Baby dolls typically have a hemline that competes with a micro-skirt for shortness, sitting at least six inches above the knee and usually short enough that underwear is visible. Baby doll dresses were launched as outerwear in 1957/58, but became popular in the 1960s and 1970s. Baby dolls are thought to be named after the 1956 movie of the same name, starring Carroll Baker.

☞ see Appliqué 23

A form of Indian embroidery that uses fine wire work to embellish garments, turbans, shoes, belts and other items. Wires are inserted into fabric and hammered flat. Badla is often used with other forms or embroidery to add richness to an item.

S/© B. Viswakumar

☛ see Embroidery 102, Shoes 218, Turban 251

Bags come in all shapes and sizes. As well as their obvious practical uses, bags can instantly make a fashion statement. Made from leather, plastic or fabric, bags can be worn over the shoulder, across the torso, on the back or simply held in the hand. Bags are perhaps the most easily accessible designer item, thanks to their relative affordability and availability through retail stores. This also makes them a useful tool for the designer, as they are a good way to advertise a brand. Louis Vuitton's hugely popular signature bags, as pictured in this image, have now become something of a status symbol and are a good example of this.

☞ see Accessories 18, Leather 151

A form of headgear with apertures for the eyes and mouth, balaclavas can be worn to cover most of the face. Balaclavas were first produced by the Balaklava village people in the Crimea during the Crimean War (1854–1856) to protect British troops from the cold temperatures. They are often associated with military forces, such as the SAS, or robbers and terrorists, as they enable the wearer to conceal their identity.

Zoe Irvin

☞ see Hats 128

A tartan cloth pattern identifying the Balfour clan, whose modern design was created by Peter MacDonald of Crieff, Perthshire, Scotland.

see Tartan 236–237

A piece of cloth tied around the head, neck or over the mouth. Bandana has been adopted into the English language, via Potuguese, from the Hindi word meaning to tie, and the often brightly-coloured garments are used for protection against sun and dust, in addition to being useful for wiping sweat away from the face. Bandanas have formed part of the ensemble worn by cowboys, pirates, farmers and more recently, gang members. Pictured is a modern interpretation of the bandana by Rudy Chandra.

Mosista Pambudi

☞ see Millinery 167, Tie 243

Zoe Irvin

A narrow piece of fabric worn around the chest as a strapless alternative to the bra. From the Old French meaning band or strip, the bandeau style has translated into swimwear and may also refer to a headband that is used to pull back the hair.

☞ see Fabric 107

The Dover Press

A close-fitting piece of lingerie that emphasises the figure. Similar in style to a corset, but allowing for freer movement, a basque extends past the waist and over the hips and often includes bra cups and detachable suspenders. As with the corset, a basque includes vertical boning or seams, and features a bodice with a lace-up or hook-and-eye fastening. Pictured is an illustration of Victorian basques, worn as part of an ensemble (above), and a contemporary basque design (right).

Zoe Irvin

☞ see Boning 46, Corset 77, Ensemble 103, Victoriana 260

Brenda Bailey

Beads that are attached to a fabric for decorative or other purposes. Beadwork can decorate the surface of a fabric or can be woven into the fabric itself. Pictured is a purse decorated with bead embroidery.

see Appliqué 23, Embroidery 102, Warp & Weft 264

A long coat, usually made of patterned black silk, worn by Hasidic Jews on the Sabbath and other Jewish holidays. Religious garments are often black because this apparent lack of colour signifies a disregard for fashion. Long garments are also often associated with religious costume as they are seen as a sign of respect and modesty.

Rob Swanson

☞ see Costume 78

A cut made diagonally, usually at a 45-degree angle, against the weave of a fabric. Garments cut on the bias often have more stretch and may appear softer than those cut on the lengthwise or crosswise grain.

Bias Cut

Zoe Irvin

☞ see Line 152, Weave 265

A two-piece swimsuit that entered popular culture following a poolside fashion show in Paris in 1946. Early bikinis were far less revealing than current versions: tops fully covered the bust and many bottoms covered the hips and upper thigh and bottoms were cut above the navel. The bikini provided much less coverage with the arrival of the string bikini in the 1970s and shrank even further by the 1980s, with the introduction of the thong bikini. The tankini, following in the tank top style, is a recent addition to the bikini family.

☞ see Tank Top 234

A process involving the wrapping of feet from infancy in order to prevent growth. Foot binding was, until recently, common practice in China, where small feet are considered very beautiful. The process was performed on girls as young as four years old and began by breaking all the toes and then tightly wrapping the feet in bandages. This process was repeated every two days and could continue for ten years, by which time the feet were only three to four inches long. Pictured are a pair of women's silk shoes from China.

see Costume 78, Shoes 218

Patterns or outlines for parts of a garment unique to a particular person. Blocks can be adapted to make patterns for different garments. Pictured is a basic block at quarter scale that includes a skirt, bodice and a sleeve. The basic shapes of the block relate to measurements of the body. For example, the hip line and bust line highlighted represent half a garment, as two of these blocks put together make an item of clothing.

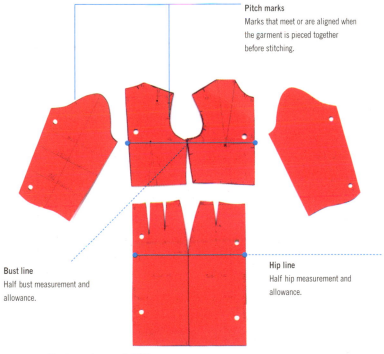

Pitch marks
Marks that meet or are aligned when the garment is pieced together before stitching.

Bust line
Half bust measurement and allowance.

Hip line
Half hip measurement and allowance.

☞ see Pattern (paper) 183

A textile printing method that applies a pattern using pressure from a wooden block inked with dye. Block printing is often performed by hand and has been practised for centuries. Designs are cut, carved or etched into blocks typically made from box, lime, holly, sycamore, plane or pear wood. Fine details are made from 'coppering' – brass or copper strips that are driven into the block surface. Printing blocks are often produced to form a repeat pattern across the surface of the textile in both the horizontal and vertical planes. Although a slow production process, block printing can produce highly creative patterns that cannot be achieved by other methods.

Elena Ray

Alexander Gitlits

A loose-fitting shirt that extends to the waist or just below. Made from cotton, silk or man-made fibres, such as polyester, a blouse features buttons on the left side, and may or may not include a collar and sleeves. Blouses tend to be more tailored than a shirt or other female garments, and often have embroidered decoration or other detailing. It is thought that the blouse originated from the Garibaldi shirt, named after Italian revolutionary Giuseppe Garibaldi, who visited England in 1863 (pictured above left).

see Collar 70, Pleats 194, Pockets 195

A corset-shaped upper garment for women, worn like a vest and usually over a blouse or chemise. A bodice may have removable sleeves or be sleeveless and is typically laced either at the back or front. The bodice was traditionally made of simple homespun fabrics and served a similar function as a brassiere. It is now associated with the folk dress of European countries. Pictured is a detail from *Die Heuernte* (The Hay-Harvest) by 19th-century artist Joseph Julien (above left) and a contemporary bodice photographed by John French (above).

☞ see Blouse 41, Chemise 66

A style of clothing inspired by Bohemian and Indian cultures, characterised by colourful, flowing garments. The word derives from the French, *bohémien*, meaning a gypsy of society, taken from the Bohemian region of Europe. In current usage a bohemian is someone who secedes from conventionality in life and in art, reflected in bohemian fashion by an apparent lack of tailoring, a mix-and-match layering of colour and texture, peasant skirts, tunics and sandals, accessorised with ethnic jewellery.

Mosista Pambudi

ChipPix

see Accessories 18, Jewellery 142, Tailoring 232

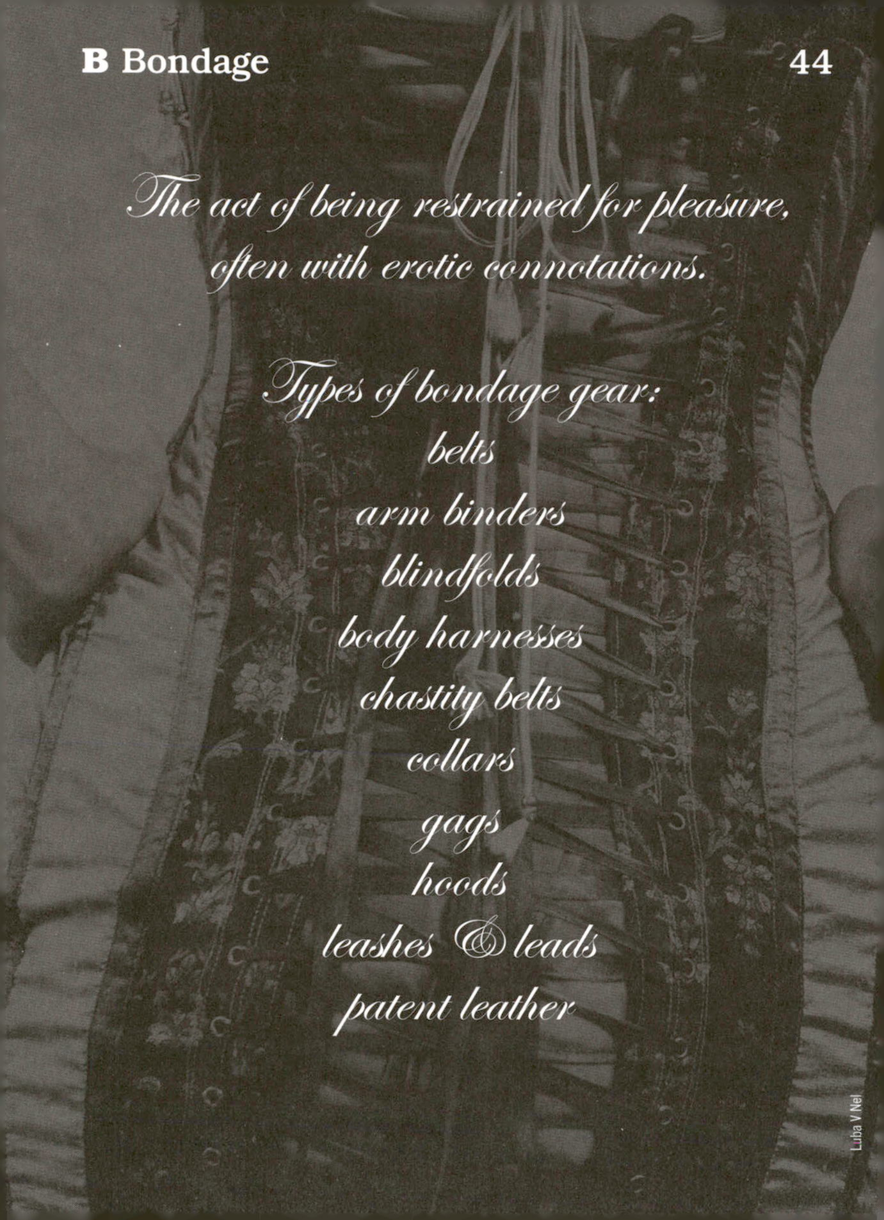

The act of being restrained for pleasure, often with erotic connotations.

Types of bondage gear:
belts
arm binders
blindfolds
body harnesses
chastity belts
collars
gags
hoods
leashes & leads
patent leather

Luba V Nel

A process by which two or more pieces of fabric are joined together to make a composite. Bonding is used to increase opacity as the different fabric layers work together to block light penetration. A bonded fabric that includes a layer of vinyl is called a laminate.

☞ see Fabric 107

Whalebone, steel, ivory, wood, cane or plastic rods inserted into sheaths that are sewn into garments to stiffen them. Boning is commonly found in clothing that serves to contour the body such as bustiers or corsets. Also called ribs or stays.

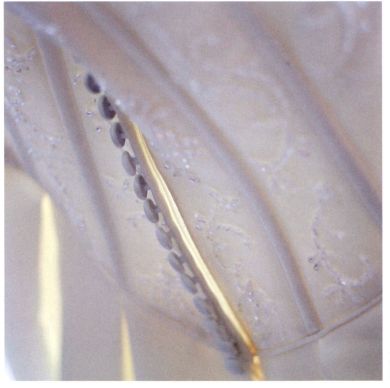

Cindy Hughes

☞ see Basque 33, Corset 77

V&A Images/Victoria and Albert Museum

A brimless hat, commonly worn in the 18th and 19th centuries. Bonnets are tied under the chin with ribbons or string and cup around the back, side and top of the head, while the brim frames the face. Summer bonnets were made from straw, with winter versions produced in heavier material, and the change from one to the other was the catalyst for the Easter Bonnet Parade. Bonnets are now more commonly associated with babies. This image shows a 1960s' take on the bonnet, photographed by John French.

☞ see Hats 128, Millinery 167

A style of jeans or trousers that tapers to the knee and slightly flares below the knee. As a result, bootleg trousers can be worn comfortably over a calf-length boot. Also called boot-cut, bootleg trousers create a flattering shape and can be worn by men and women.

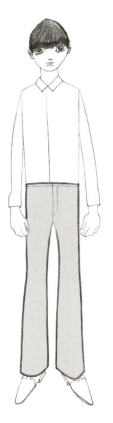

A type of durable footwear that also covers the leg; worn for protection, hygiene and style for several hundred years. Various different styles are in common usage:

Cowboy
A high, arched boot with Cuban heel and ornamental stitching that is traditionally a work boot worn by cowboys. Normally made from leather, however, snake, alligator and lizard skin are also used.

Go-go
A boot created in the 1960s to be worn for dancing, often worn with a miniskirt or dress and popularised by Nancy Sinatra in the song *These Boots Are Made For Walking*.

Kinky
A full-length boot with high heels that extends to the thigh or crotch, typically produced in patent leather or PVC in bright colours and often associated with dominatrix or fetishism.

Knee high
A boot rising to just below the knee and tight around the leg and ankle. It may be fastened with laces, buckles or a zip, or can simply be pulled on.

Platform
A boot with a thick sole or a combination of a thick sole and high heel, which is often brightly coloured and glitzy. Popularised by glam rockers in the 1970s, platform boots are also part of the wardrobe of the cyber subculture.

Ugg
A boot made from sheepskin with a fleece lining and flat sole, originating in Australia as a type of slipper to protect against the cold. Ugg boots are typically worn with jeans.

terekhov igor

A retail outlet that specialises in fashion or jewellery. A boutique (from the French word for small shop) tends to sell clothing created by a particular designer (or limited range of designers), rather than clothes produced for the mass market, although this distinction is now blurring. Pictured is the storefront of the boutique of English designer Alexander McQueen. Clothes from McQueen's collection can be seen displayed on mannequins in the window, with the brand name above the door.

Xavier Young

☞ **see Mannequin 159**

A symbol, mark, word or phrase that identifies and differentiates a product, service or organisation from its competitors. Brands are created to help us distinguish between similar product offerings, through perceptions of quality and value. Brands act as a recognisable symbol for a certain level of quality, frequently aiding our purchase decision. Pictured is a loose broadsheet brochure, created by Sagmeister Inc. design studio for New York designer Anni Kuan, which hangs on a coat wire and features a burn created by a hot iron.

Brassiere or Bra:

An article of underwear designed to lift and support the bust, the bra consists of cups, centre panel, band running around the torso and usually two shoulder straps. Bra is an abbreviation of the word brassiere, itself from the French, *brassière,* meaning bodice or child's vest.
The contemporary bra design was patented by American Mary Phelps-Jacobs in 1914 and consisted of two silk handkerchiefs tied together with ribbon to make straps. Cup sizes were introduced in 1935 and the development of synthetic fibres, such as nylon, Lycra and polyester have seen bras become more lightweight, flexible and seamless. Many types of bra now exist and have different functions, support capability and visual appearance. However, an estimated 80% of women wear the wrong sized bra.

Types of bra:

Full cup, Balcony, Half cup, Quarter cup, Push up,
Plunge, Underwired, Soft cup, Multiway,
Strapless, Maternity,
Sports.

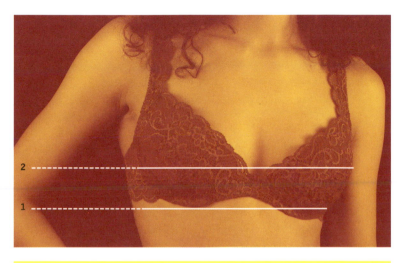

Code	AA	A	B	C	D	E	F	FF	G	GG	H	HH	J	JJ
Cup size [cm]	10–12	12–14	14–16	16–18	18–20	13	15	18	20	23	26	28	30	32.5
Cup size [inch]	0 to 0.5	0.5 to 1	1 to 2	2 to 3	3 to 4	7	8	7	8	9	10	11	12	13

Code letters that relate to a given cup size. Bra size is determined by three measurements, although garments produced by different manufacturers vary a great deal. The frame size or underband is a tight measure around the torso and directly under the breasts (**1**). Add five inches if this is an odd number or four inches if it is even. Bust size is measured around the chest (**2**), including the fullest part of the breasts. Cup size is the difference between bust and frame sizes and is converted into a letter as per the table (above).

A trouser-like garment worn by men from the late 16th to early 19th centuries. Breeches have varied in length but are typically fastened just below the knee. This image shows a coat, breeches and waistcoat ensemble from England. Notice how the breeches fit tightly just below the knee.

V&A Images./Victoria and Albert Museum

see Coat 68, Waistcoat 263

Materials used to produce the dress, veil and related garments that comprise a wedding outfit. Bridalwear tends to use the richest, boldest fabrics within the budget available, such as silk and satin either with a plain or floral design. In Western culture, wedding dresses tend to be white, ivory, cream or similar neutral colours – a tradition that is commonly credited to the wedding of Queen Victoria of England and Albert of Saxe-Coburg and Gotha in 1840.

THE MARRIAGE OF QUEEN VICTORIA AND PRINCE ALBERT OF SAXE-COBURG AND GOTHA AT ST JAMES'S PALACE, FEBRUARY 10, 1840.

Left: The 1840 wedding of Queen Victoria and Prince Albert, which began the vogue for white bridalwear.

Below left: A highly decorated design by Michael Woodward.

Below centre: Detail of a bridal gown by Gordana Sermek.

Below right: A simpler design by Gordana Sermek.

Michael Woodward

Gordana Sermek

Gordana Sermek

☞ **see Garment 118**

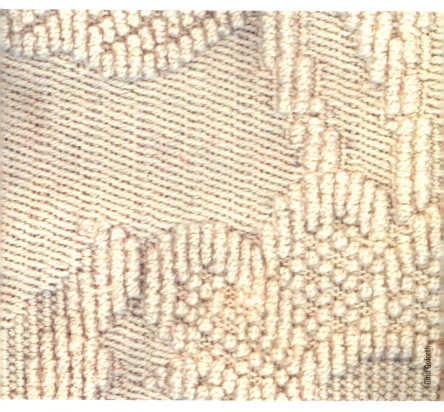

Gina Goforth

Rich, heavy fabric with a raised, shuttle-woven design. Often made with coloured silks and may feature gold and silver threads. Floral, foliage, scrollwork or pastoral scenes are common motifs. Brocade is commonly used for curtains, pillows, wraps and church vestments.

see Fabric 107

A form of decorating white cotton or linen. Broderie anglaise features rows of cutwork with embroidered edges to form floral shapes and patterns bound with buttonhole stitches. Pictured is a photograph by John French featuring a model wearing a broderie anglaise slip.

V&A Images/Victoria and Albert Museum

☞ see Embroidery 102

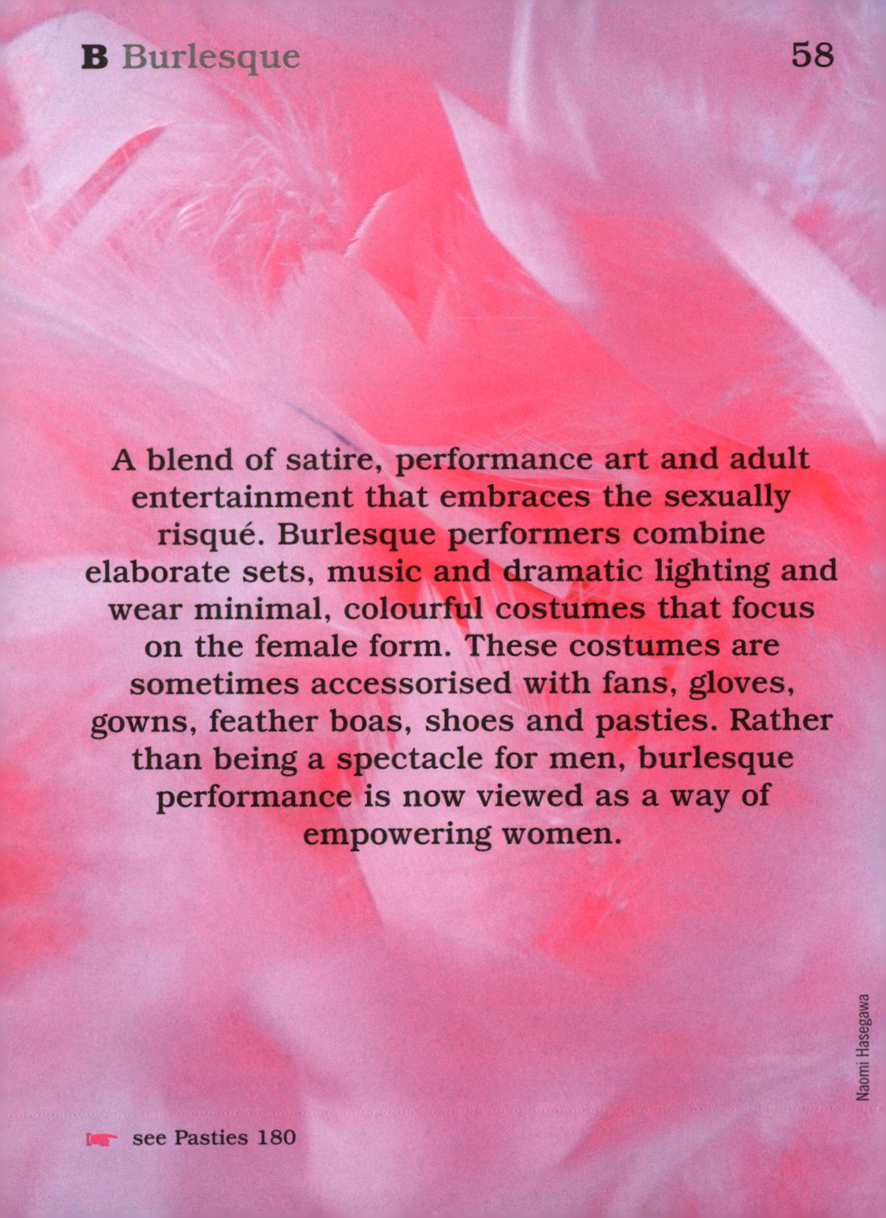

A blend of satire, performance art and adult entertainment that embraces the sexually risqué. Burlesque performers combine elaborate sets, music and dramatic lighting and wear minimal, colourful costumes that focus on the female form. These costumes are sometimes accessorised with fans, gloves, gowns, feather boas, shoes and pasties. Rather than being a spectacle for men, burlesque performance is now viewed as a way of empowering women.

Naomi Hasegawa

see Pasties 180

Jose Manuel Gelpi Diaz

A loose black or light blue robe that covers the body from head to toe, worn by some Muslim women. A full burqa conceals the entire face save for a veiled eye hole. However, burquas can be worn to expose the eyes, as shown here, or the entire face. A burqa (or burka) is usually worn over a long dress or salwar kameez.

A small disc or knob-shaped device attached to an article of clothing for utilitarian or decorative purposes. Typically used to fasten an opening, the button is passed through a slit in the fabric (called a buttonhole) or a thread loop. Buttons are sized in lignes, abbreviated to L, with 40 lignes measuring one inch. Materials used in the manufacture of buttons include bone, horn, ivory, shell, wood, glass, metal and plastic. Buttons became more commonplace with the form-fitting garments of 13th- and 14th-century Europe.

marymary

☞ see Fastenings 109

A coarse, lightweight fabric made from unbleached cotton using a plain weave and low thread count. Calico originates from Calicut in Kerala, India and is typically printed with brightly coloured designs, either by discharge or resist printing. Calico is often used to make toiles, due to its relative cheapness.

☞ see Toile 244

Dana Heinemann

A short, sleeveless undergarment for women, similar to
a vest, covering the top of the body, but with skinnier
straps. Camisole derives from the Latin, *camisia*, for
shirt or nightgown. Camisoles are produced in silk,
satin, cotton, nylon and Lycra and are often used for
layering and can be worn with jeans. Some camisole
tops are produced with built-in bust support to
eliminate the need for a bra.

see Bra 52, Lingerie 153

Women's calf-length trousers created by Italian designer Emilio Pucci in 1949 and first sold in his boutique on the island of Capri just off the coast of Naples in Italy. They are also sometimes called pedal pushers or clam diggers, though there are some subtle distinctions between these: Capris are a slimline pant ending just below the knee, usually with a small inverted v at the hem on the side to ease movement. Pedal pushers give a looser fit and are longer, as they end at the calf. Clam diggers also extend to the calf, but are baggier. Once just for women, calf-length trousers are now also worn by men.

Zoe Irvin

Natalia Mikhaylova

A knitted, woollen garment similar to a sweater or jacket, but with an opening down the front, which can be fastened with buttons or a zip. A cardigan can be worn by men or women and is named after British military commander, James Thomas Brudenell, seventh earl of Cardigan (1797–1868) (pictured above left), who led the charge of the Light Brigade at the Battle of Balaclava.

☞ see Balaclava 29

A long platform upon which models parade garments from new clothing collections at fashion shows.

Kateryna Potrokhova

see Model 171

V&A Images/Victoria and Albert Museum

A simple, smock-like garment with sleeves, but no collar or cuffs. Chemises became popular in the Middle Ages when women wore them under gowns or robes and men under doublets and robes. Typically made from finely woven cotton, linen or silk, they are essentially a loose-fitting, straight-hanging dress without a waist. Pictured is a ladies' cotton shift or chemise and cotton drawers from England, c.1834.

Stylish or smart. Chic (a French word adopted by the British) is often used to describe how individual garments or ensembles make a person look, but what is and what is not chic is difficult to define. Chic refers to someone who wears stylish clothes with ease and whose outfit is arresting, modern and elegant. Anne Gunning, photographed here by John French, appears chic in this figure-hugging velveteen evening coat, which creates an elegant, elongated profile accentuated by her tied-back hair and contrasting white gloves and hat.

V&A Images/Victoria and Albert Museum

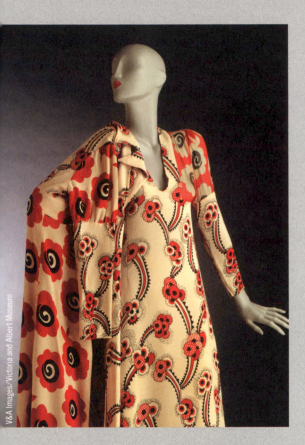

V&A Images/Victoria and Albert Museum

Outerwear worn by men and women over an outfit to provide protection from the elements. A coat is usually at least thigh length, with long sleeves and a front opening, which may be fastened with buttons, zips, poppers, toggles or belts. Coats provide thermal insulation and are often waterproof. Coats are available in many styles, such as a great coat, duffel coat, trench coat or fur coat. Pictured is an evening dress and coat created by English designer Ossie Clark (a leading designer from 1964–1974).

☞ see Duffel 96, Macintosh 156, Trench Coat 249

A dress worn by women at cocktail parties, semi-formal and formal occasions, with a form-fitting waist and skirt extending to anywhere from just above the knee to about two inches above the ankle, known as tea length. Cocktail dresses may be simply or richly decorated and use a variety of exquisite materials such as silk, satin and chiffon. A variation of the cocktail dress is the LBD ('Little Black Dress') created in the 1920s by Coco Chanel, which was designed to fit any woman and not show any stains. These black dresses are versatile and can be worn dressed up or down.

Zoe Irvin

☞ see Collection 71, Dress 95, Tea Length 239

Part of a shirt or blouse that fastens around the neck. Collars take a variety of forms that serve both decorative and functional purposes. The adoption of the tie led to shirts with fold-over collars, which often include stiffeners inserted into the fabric to prevent the points from turning up.

Ascot collar Worn with a cravat, a tall collar with points turned up over the chin.

Barrymore collar A turnover collar with long or tapered points that was popular in the 1970s.

Buttoned-down collar The collar points are buttoned down to the body of the shirt.

Convertible collar The neck button can be worn either fastened or unfastened.

Detachable collar Introduced in the mid-16th century – probably to allow for starching and finishing.

Gladstone collar Popularised by Prime Minister William Ewart Gladstone, the points were pressed to stand out horizontally at the sides.

Peter Pan collar Flat with rounded corners, popular for women in the mid-20th century.

Poet collar A soft collar with long points, typical of that worn by poets like Byron and Shelley.

Windsor collar Slightly stiffened with a wide gap between the points in order to accommodate the Windsor knot tie.

Wing A small standing collar with points that stick out horizontally worn with men's evening dress of white tie or black tie.

Above: British politician William Ewart Gladstone (1798–1869) was a strong advocate for the abolition of capital punishment and is pictured here wearing a 'Gladstone collar'.

☞ see 9, Tie 243

Portfolio of a designer's best work, often organised seasonally. All the garments in a collection represent the designer's inspiration and usually explore common themes, textiles, textures and colours.

☞ see Season 214, Theme 241

A circular representation of the colour spectrum that provides a visual reference for helping to select colour combinations. The colour wheel helps to explain the relationship between different colours within colour theory, it illustrates the classification of colours and provides a quick reference to the primary, secondary and tertiary hues, which can help a designer successfully select functional colour schemes. Colours have certain associations in fashion. Black can be variously associated with power, evil, ultra chic, the gothic subculture and the bad-boy leather-clad rebel. By contrast, white is thought to represent purity in the West and is used for wedding dresses, but it is also a neutral colour used for dress shirts.

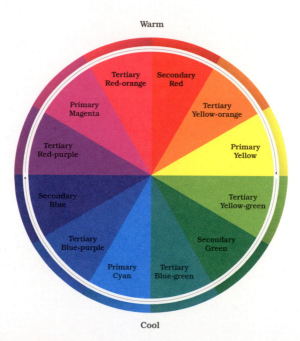

Using the colour wheel, a designer can select harmonious colour combinations, such as complementary or contrasting colours, which face each other on the wheel, or triads, any three colours that are equidistant from one another. In any design, a dominant colour is usually supported by subordinate and accent colours.

Monochrome
Any single colour on the wheel.

Complementary
Colours that face each other on the wheel. These provide strong contrast and so their use will result in a more vibrant design. Also called contrasting colours.

Split complements
Three colours that comprise the two adjacent colours to the (unselected) colour that is complementary to the principle colour selection.

Triads
Triads are any three colours that are equidistant on the colour wheel. As all three colours contrast with one another, this provides a visual tension. The primary and secondary colour spaces are triads.

Analogous
The two colours on either side of a principle colour selection. Analogous colours provide a harmonious and natural blend.

Mutual complements
A triad of equidistant colours together with the complementary colour of the central one of the three.

Near complements
A colour adjacent to the complementary colour of the principle colour selection.

Double complements
Any two adjacent colours and their two complements.

The central and overriding idea or motif presented in a design or through an overall clothing collection. A concept represents the thinking behind a design that is the starting point and constant reference. A concept may be prominently or subtly presented and can be as simple as Africa, burlesque or pirate, to name a few examples. Pictured is an invite created for designer Alexander McQueen by Mono Design. The design carries a circus concept and features a clown image and the legend 'merry go round'. This legend refers to the fun event that the recipient is being invited to, and perhaps comments on the fashion industry itself.

☞ see Collection 71, Theme 241

A colour palette in which the different hues stand out against each other. Contrasting colours can be used to create vivid fabric designs, such as the Chanel ensemble (1937–1938) pictured. Some colour combinations project and are more contrasting as shown in the panels below. Yellow and cyan project from and contrast with red, while magenta recedes into it.

In traditional dressmaking, the bodice or waist of a dress, such as those in the illustration, to which the skirts are attached. A corsage is often confused with a corset, perhaps in part because a bridal corset is a corsage. Corsage also refers to a small bouquet of flowers that may be attached to a dress or placed around the wrist.

The Dover Press

☞ see Corset 77

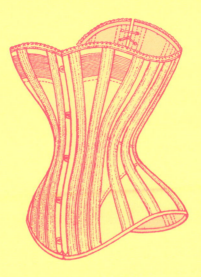

A lace-up garment stiffened by boning and worn around the torso to mould the body into a desired shape. Originally worn by men and women, corsets were used to constrict the waist and reduce its size, known as tight-lacing (with a waist of 13 inches possible in extreme cases), and were worn over a chemise or shift during the Victorian era. The corset has evolved into a women's garment that mimics the look without actually performing the body shaping function (although they still maintain boning and lacing features), as it has become an item of outerwear.

☞ see Basque 33, Boning 46, Victoriana 260

Top left: Classical Khmer dancers at Angkor Wat, Cambodia.

Above: A Muslim girl from Karachi, Pakistan wearing a salwar and blouse (c.1870).

Far left: A woman from Norway wearing the rural Bunad costume.

Left: A Japanese woman dressed in a kimono (c.1870).

A style of dress identified with a particular era, class, community or region. Before fashions became global and widespread one could often predict where people came from and what they did by the clothes they wore. The use of kimonos in Japan, the mantilla lace or silk scarf worn over the head and shoulders by women in Spain, and the Scottish kilt are all examples of costume. Many of these traditional costumes have fallen out of use on a daily basis and now only appear during cultural celebrations or on festive days.

see Kilt 145, Kimono 146

A scarf or band of fabric worn by men around the neck in a slipknot, with long ends overlapping at the front. The cravat is often thought to be the forerunner to the modern tie. They first entered Parisian culture in the 1630s, when Croatian mercenaries supporting King Louis XIII against Duc de Guise and Marie de Medici, wore the distinct neckties as part of their military kit. The style reached British shores with Charles II in 1660 when he returned from exile, but nowadays cravats tend to be reserved for special occasions, such as weddings. Pictured is a jumper by Elsa Schiaparelli from the early 20th century with a cravat design in the knit.

V&A Images/Victoria and Albert Museum

☛ see Collar 70, Tie 243

A stiffened petticoat structure designed to support the skirts of a woman's dress, which eventually evolved into caged or hooped underskirt frames. During the 1840s flounces and pleats gave full skirts the illusion of greater width, but as the decade progressed and more petticoats were added to create an even broader shape, the 'required' minimum of six petticoats was heavy, bulky, hot and uncomfortable. The caged crinoline was patented in 1856 by American W. S. Thomson and had steel hoops attached to vertical tapes that descended from a band around the wearer's waist. The crinoline gave the required bell shape, but reduced the need for so many layers of petticoats, thus making the outfit lighter and allowing for freer leg movement. But with a maximum diameter of 180cm (six feet) a crinoline could be awkward to manoeuvre and a gust of wind could reveal more leg than was considered decent. By 1864 the crinoline was modified and the dome shape disappeared; the front and sides were contracted in favour of volume at the rear, for example, the bustle.

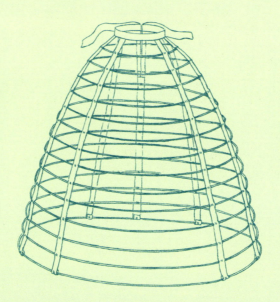

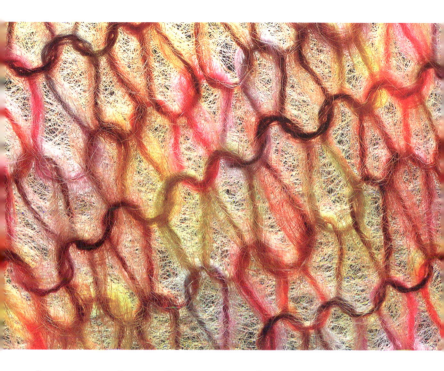

A method using cord, yarn, thread or wire to create a fabric. From the Middle French, *croc* or *croche*, meaning to hook, crocheting involves placing a slipknot loop over a hook, pulling another loop through the first one, and repeating to create a chain. Crocheting became popular in the 1830s and continues to be used to make bags, hats and shawls.

Hannu Liivaar

☞ see Knitting 148

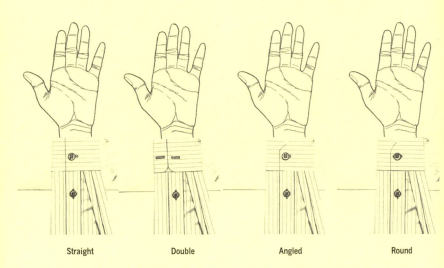

Straight   Double   Angled   Round

A turned-back extension at the end of a shirt sleeve, or a separate band of material sewn on to the end of a shirt sleeve. Button cuffs are fastened by buttoning one or more buttons on one side of the cuff through the other side to close it around the wrist. French cuffs are fastened with cufflinks: a pair of decorative fastenings that have a short chain or post that passes through the buttonholes, and can be found in numerous variations of construction and design. In the USA, a cuff also refers to a turn-up on a trouser leg.

Anthony Fourrier

A broad, pleated waist sash worn with black tie underneath a dinner jacket. From the Urdu and Persian *kamar-band*, from *kamar*, meaning waist or loins and *bandi*, meaning band, the cummerbund was adopted by the British military in India during colonial times. The horizontal pleats were often worn facing up so that they could hold tickets.

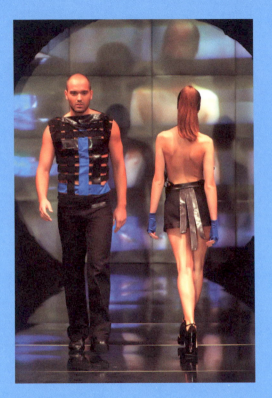

Gordana Sermek

A subculture that developed around trance and hardcore electronic music. Cyber fashion is a mixture of rave and goth and draws on Japanese anime, with the use of contrasting colours such as red, black, white and those that reflect ultraviolet light. Body piercing, hair extensions and boots with thick soles that extend up the calf are also commonly associated with cyber fashion.

☞ see Anime 22, Piercing 188, Subcultures 228

A reversible, self-patterned fabric produced from silk, wool, linen, cotton or man-made fibres. Different weave structures in the warp and weft create patterns by reflecting light. First produced in China, its production spread westwards through India and Persia, but was named after the Syrian city of Damascus in the 12th century due to the beauty of the designs produced there. Pictured is a selection of swatches of 14th-century Italian silk damask.

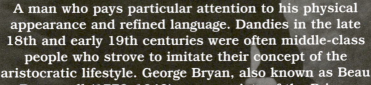

A man who pays particular attention to his physical appearance and refined language. Dandies in the late 18th and early 19th centuries were often middle-class people who strove to imitate their concept of the aristocratic lifestyle. George Bryan, also known as Beau Brummell (1778–1840), an associate of the Prince Regent, obtained celebrity status as a Dandy, due to his wit and immaculate presentation. Dandies often appear in fiction in strong roles. The Scarlet Pimpernel portrays himself as an irrelevant dandy in his public life in order to draw attention away from his true identity, a charade also used by the fictional spy Austin Powers.

Pamela Moore

A sewn fold in the construction of a garment to shape fabric to the curves of the body such as the bust, waist and hip areas.

☞ see Garment 118

The exploration of clothing structure where garments may be literally taken apart in some way and put back together unfinished, inside out or deteriorating. Fashion designer, Vivienne Westwood was a pioneer of the punk look, an early manifestation of deconstruction in fashion. The trend shows an unwillingness to conform to 'regular' or accepted ways of dressing. During the early 1980s, John Galliano's collections included jackets worn upside down and inside out. Deconstructed clothes continue in contemporary designs and rely on faded, ripped or torn fabrics without finish and with frayed edges. The outfit in the image could be described as deconstructed due to the treatment of the fabric with irregular seams, lack of colour and absence of the second arm that we would expect to see.

see Punk 201

Gina Smith

A hat worn for hunting in rural areas, featuring brims fore and aft to provide sun protection and flexible side flaps that can be worn tied up or down to protect the ears in cold weather. The pattern, in muted brown tones, provides camouflage. The deerstalker was popularised in films about the fictional detective Sherlock Holmes, although he never wore one in the works by Arthur Conan Doyle.

☞ see Hats 128

Durable, cotton fabric, primarily used to make jeans. The word 'denim' is a contraction of *serge de Nîmes* – serge (a durable twilled, woollen or worsted fabric), from Nîmes (a town in France). Identified by a diagonal ribbing on the reverse (created by passing the weft under two or more warp fibres), denim is traditionally dyed with the blue pigment obtained from indigo dye. Since the late 19th century a synthetic substitute has been used instead.

During the Californian Gold Rush, miners required hard-wearing clothes that would not tear easily. In 1853 Leob Strauss began a wholesale business meeting the miners' needs. He later changed his name and Levi Strauss & Co. remains one of the top denim clothing producers today.

☞ see Dye 98, Warp & Weft 264

Vladislav Gurfinkel

Fabric that has been artificially aged or worn. Distressing fabric is a technique used to create clothing with a range of visual appearances by using abrasives to wear the surface of the cloth. It is commonly used to age the appearance of denim and reduce the intensity of the indigo dye. In addition to varying the visual presentation of a pair of jeans, aging them in this manner also reduces their life span.

Dana Heinemann

A layered look with one T-shirt or other garment worn over another. A double-tee top can have either harmonious or contrasting colours to create different visual impacts. This illustration shows a contrasting combination.

see Colour Wheel Selections 73

Zoe Irvin

Narrow trousers in denim or non-stretchable material that closely hug the leg. Drainpipe trousers were worn by Teddy boys in the UK in the 1950s and by punks in the 1970s. As with many other aspects of fashion, trouser leg tightness changes frequently.

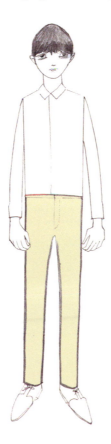

Anthony Fourrier

see Punk 201

V&A Images/Victoria and Albert Museum

A garment made from unstitched cloth that is held to the body with some kind of fastening. Draped garments include togas, saris, sarongs, shawls, capes and mantles, such as the six-yard-long Robe of State that formed part of the coronation robes of Queen Elizabeth II, as pictured in this photograph by Cecil Beaton. The crimson velvet mantle is edged with ermine and two rows of handmade embroidered gold lace and gold filigree work and was made by Messrs Ede & Ravenscroft of Chancery Lane, London.

☞ see Embroidery 102, Garment 118

A garment consisting of a skirt with attached (or matching) bodice, giving the effect of a one-piece garment. A dress, frock or gown is typically worn by women and is made from light- to mid-weight fabrics such as denim, jersey, worsted, or poplin although other materials such as silk, satin, wool and velvet are also used. Fashion plays a determining factor in prevailing hemline lengths. Pictured is a velvet cocktail dress (1969) designed by Valentino, featuring cap sleeves and a cummerbund of braid embroidered with diamantés.

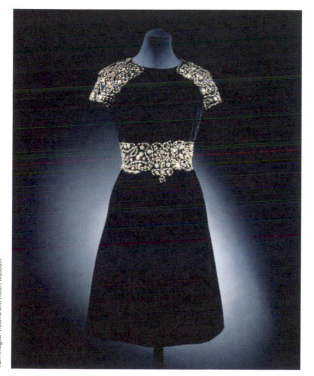

V&A Images/Victoria and Albert Museum

☞ see Cocktail Dress 69, Cummerbund 83, Eveningwear 106

Heavy woollen cloth named after a town in Belgium, where the cloth was originally made, which is used to produce bags and overcoats, such as that made famous by the fictional children's character Paddington Bear.

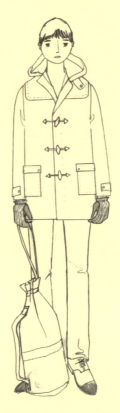

Anthony Fourrier

☞ see Coat 68

A mould of the human form that is used for draping fabrics and making clothes. Also called a tailor's dummy, the different parts on some models can be moved to approximate different body sizes. This should not be confused with a mannequin, which is used to display clothes in a retail environment.

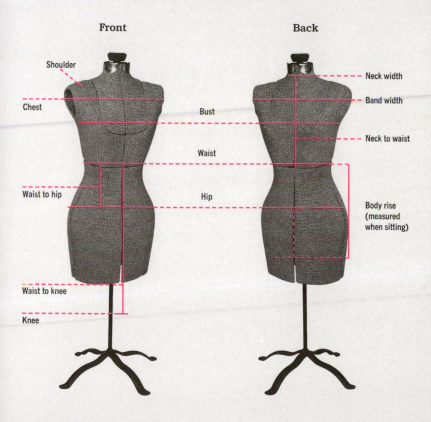

Front

Back

Shoulder

Chest

Bust

Waist

Waist to hip

Hip

Waist to knee

Knee

Neck width

Band width

Neck to waist

Body rise (measured when sitting)

☞ see Mannequin 159

A substance applied to fabric in order to change its colour. Before the development of chemical dyes, plant and animal extracts were used, which meant the colour palette available was dependent on locally available materials. This made certain colours synonymous with certain regions, such as the blue used for robes worn by the Hmong people in Northern Vietnam, which comes from the *indigofera tinctoria* indigo plant.

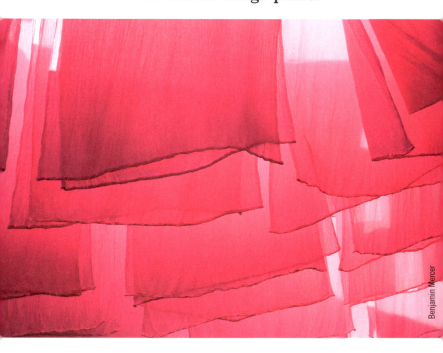

Benjamin Mercer

Known as the *Belle Epoque* (fine period) throughout Europe, the period from 1901–1910 when Edward VII reigned in England was one of luxurious living. The fashionable hour-glass figure depended on tight corsets and lily-like skirts, while necks lowered, allowing the display of jewellery and lace adornments. Feathers, gloves, wide-brim hats, parasols and bags were also essential items in the Edwardian lady's wardrobe. For men, the growing popularity of motoring, sport and outdoor pursuits meant that clothing became more practical, with tweeds and heavier fabrics used for everyday and country wear suits. This photograph by Andrew Pitcairn-Knowles, taken in Ostend, Belgium, c.1900, depicts a mother and daughter in Edwardian dress.

V&A Images/Victoria and Albert Museum

A stretchable fabric created using small pieces of masticated rubber, developed by Thomas Hancock, founder of the British rubber industry. Elastic describes the ability of the cloth tape to return to its original shape when a load is removed and Hancock used his invention to create fastenings for gloves, suspenders, shoes and stockings, which he patented in 1820. Elastic was revolutionary because it allowed clothes that could cling to the body without falling down to be developed. This, in turn, saw it become a key material component in clothing manufacture.

Branislav Ostojic

The period in England between 1558–1603, at the time of Elizabeth I's reign and the height of the English Renaissance. Rich, heavy velvets, jewels, furs, satins and taffeta in stiff, exaggerated shapes created by padding and quilting epitomised the fashions of this time. Bodices came to a point at the waist and had separate sleeves that were ruffed at the shoulders and fastened with lace. Skirts were full with circular frames. Men wore tight waists and sometimes wore corsets to obtain the wasp-waisted look. Pictured is a dress detail by Madame Vignon, made in Elizabethan style of cerise taffeta and silk, from 1869–70.

V&A Images/Victoria and Albert Museum

☞ see Petticoat 186

Iurii Konoval

A method of decorating fabric with designs stitched in coloured thread or yarn using a needle. Embroidery may also see other materials sewn on to the surface of the cloth, such as beads and sequins. Embroidery can be performed in several ways, with or without a design, and has been practised by many generations all over the world.

see Appliqué 23, Beading 34, Broderie Anglaise 57, Fabric 107

An outfit made of separate but coordinated garments. Pictured is an ensemble by British designer Jean Muir from the late 20th century.

V&A Images/Victoria and Albert Museum

☞ see Costume 78, Garment 118

A removable ornamental shoulder piece that displays insignia or designates rank in the military and other organisations. Epaulettes, a diminutive from the French, *épaule*, meaning shoulder, are fastened to a shoulder strap that runs parallel to the shoulder seam and buttons near the collar. Epaulettes may be fringed.

see Collar 70

An aesthetic focus on sexual desire, particularly related to the anticipation of sexual activity and the attempt to incite feelings of desire. The term derives from Eros, the Ancient Greek god of love, and is viewed as sensual love or the libido. In fashion, garments such as fetish wear and certain pieces of lingerie are intentionally designed to arouse desire. Some garments are considered more erotic than others, such as the long gloves pictured.

Mayer George Vladimirovich

V&A Images/Victoria and Albert Museum

An ensemble suitable for formal events. Eveningwear for men is either a white tie with tailcoat or black tie with a dinner jacket or tuxedo. Women may wear a ballgown, evening gown or cocktail dress. An evening gown is typically a long, loose-fitting garment in silk, velvet, satin or chiffon, ranging from tea length to full length. Pictured is an evening dress created by Jean Muir (1996).

see Cocktail Dress 69, Dress 95, Skirt Length 222, Tuxedo 253

Any material made by weaving, knitting, crocheting, or bonding yarns or threads to form a textile. Fabric or cloth is available in many different varieties, including those below.

Lamé
A woven fabric using metallic gold or silver yarns, often used for eveningwear as tissue lamé, hologram lamé and pearl lamé.

Burlap
A dense, coarse, woven fabric made of jute or other vegetable fibres, which is strong and inexpensive, often used for sacking. Also called hessian.

Lace
A lightweight fabric patterned with open holes where cotton or other thread is looped, twisted or braided to other threads independent from a backing fabric.

Gingham
A fabric made from dyed cotton warp yarns. Originally a stripped fabric, it became checked in the 18th century when production started in Manchester.

Velvet
A tufted fabric made from silk, cotton or synthetic fibres with evenly distributed cut threads to give a short, dense pile.

Corduroy
A textile of twisted fibres that lay parallel when woven, forming parallel ribs or cords called wales.

Jersey
A knitted fabric with a definite smooth side that faces out on garments and a textured inside.

Organza
A thin, plain-weave, sheer fabric made from silk or synthetic fibres, often used for bridal and eveningwear.

Tweed
A rough, unfinished woollen fabric with plain or twill weave and check, twill or herringbone pattern, used for outerwear due to its durability and moisture resistance.

The changing tastes and trends that over time are regenerated and repeated. Dress hemlines go up, down and up again as the fashion cycle and zeitgeist change and people look for the fresh and new. Inspiration for new fashions often comes from revisiting and reusing the fads and fashions from previous decades in a cycle, such as Laver's Law, developed by James Laver in *Taste and Fashion* in 1945, and showing how people's reaction to a fashion change and mellow over time.

Indecent	10 years before its time
Shameless	5 years before its time
Outré	1 year before its time
Smart	–
Dowdy	1 year after its time
Hideous	10 years after its time
Ridiculous	20 years after its time
Amusing	30 years after its time
Quaint	40 years after its time
Charming	70 years after its time
Romantic	100 years after its time
Beautiful	150 years after its time

☞ see Inspiration 138, Zeitgeist 271

Zip
A device invented by Elias Howe in 1851 for temporarily joining two edges of fabric by interlocking metal or plastic teeth.

Button
A small disc or knob on a garment that passes through a fabric or thread loop to hold two pieces of fabric together.

Velcro
A hook-and-loop system that sticks on contact, invented by Georges de Mestral in 1941 and based on burdock seeds. Velcro is a contraction of the French *velours* (velvet) and *croché* (hooked).

Rivet
A permanent, two-piece metal fastener commonly used to fix the pockets of denim jeans.

Buckle
A metal clasp used to retain the end of a strap. From the Latin, *buccula*, buckles were commonly used on boots before the zip was invented.

Hook and eye
A blunt, metal hook that is inserted into a loop or eyelet, typically used on boots during the Victorian era. Hooks are also used with shoelaces for fastening boots.

Tie side
A bikini, dress or top that has strings or straps that tie at the side.

Frogging
A braided button and loop that provide an ornamental garment fastening. Also called frog button or Chinese frog due to its use on oriental clothes.

Press studs
A pair of interlocking metal discs used in place of buttons that fasten clothing with a snapping sound. Also called snap fastener or popper, they are easier for children to use than buttons.

A soft felt hat invented in the 1910s with a curled brim, lengthwise crease down the crown and pinched front on both sides. Named after the heroine of an 1882 play by Victorien Sardou, who wore a similar hat, the fedora or trilby can also be made from straw and twill. Popular in the early 20th century, the fedora provided climate protection, while being compact enough to wear in a car.

☞ see Hats 128

A psychological disorder of a fixation on an inanimate object, body part or feature, or sexual practice. Fetish clothing is designed to create sexual arousal and satisfaction and can range from corsets, skin-tight rubber, gloves and footwear (such as the boots in this illustration), to more extreme items such as collars, bondage masks and leather harnesses. Materials commonly used in fetish gear include leather, rubber, spandex and plastics like PVC and vinyl.

Michel Isola

see Bondage 44, Eroticism 105

A red felt hat shaped like a truncated cone with a black tassel, originating in Fez, Morocco, also called a tarboosh. Pictured is an Egyptian stamp featuring King Farouk I wearing a fez.

☞ see Hats 128

A loose-fitting shift dress with little shape and no sleeves, the flapper dress tended to be calf-length and with a waistline dropped to the hips. The flapper characterised the mid- to late 1920s, and the Charleston- and jazz-inspired hedonism of the 'roaring twenties'. The flapper dress allowed women greater movement while dancing and also presented elegant lines. Pictured is a dress by Voisin, France (c.1925).

Unspun natural fibres from the flax, common flax or linseed plant *linum usitatissimum*. Flax is a soft, flexible and lustrous fibre that is stronger, but less elastic than cotton and is used to produce linen fabrics like damask and lace. Flax is one of the oldest fibre crops in the world – production and usage was first carried out 5,000 years ago with the domestication of the plant in the Fertile Crescent in the Middle East.

☞ see Fabric 107, Natural Fibres 175

The Dover Press

Fabric printed with flower motifs, such as those popularised by 19th-century designer, William Morris, and more recently by retailer Laura Ashley. Bohemian-style dresses with floral prints in earth tones were particularly popular during the 1970s.

☞ see Block Printing 40, Bohemian 43, Print 198

The materials used in the production of shoes that provide protective, performance and/or decorative functions. Footwear composition affects the fit, durability and look of a shoe.

Upper
Part of a shoe that covers the upper foot surface, commonly made from leather, plastic, fabric or rubber.

Lining and Sock
The inner surface of the shoe upper, which may be full or partial. such as just in the heel.

Outer Sole
The bottom of a shoe, attached to the upper and in contact with the ground.

Leather
Hide or skin that retains its original fibrous structure.

Coated Leather
Treated hide or skin that retains its original fibrous structure, but will not rot after absorbing water.

Textile
Fabric used to produce uppers, such as canvas.

Other Materials
Plastic, rubber, silk or any other material used in shoe production.

☞ see Leather 151, Shoes 218

PARFUMD'ETE

Guido Mocafico

Perfume produced from essential oils, aroma compounds and other elements to provide a pleasing and attractive smell. Fragrance production has become a cornerstone of the fashion industry with all major designers and labels extending their brands to include a range of perfumes and aftershaves. Pictured is a bottle design created by Research Studios for Kenzo.

see Boutique 50, Brand 51

G Garment

A garment is a piece of clothing made up of various pieces of fabric and fastenings. It is the variation in the style of these elements that defines different fashions.

Collar

Yoke

Lapel

Lapel hole or buttonhole

Pocket

Single-breasted

Sleeve

Button / buttonhole

Cuff

Camp pockets
Squared, seamed pockets sewn to the outside of the garment.

Vent

Waistband

Carriers or belt loops

Fly front / fly

Rivet

Fifth pocket or 'watch pocket'

Turn up

Hip pocket
Pocket sewn on the front of a garment at hip height.

Seam

Hem

Jurgita Genyte

A loop of cloth used to hold stockings up. In its modern form, garters are decorative lace, silk and ribbon accessories, often worn by women underneath their wedding dresses as part of a tradition involving taking off part of the bride's clothing to bring good luck. However, before the discovery of elastic in Elizabethan times, leather or heavy cloth garters were worn just below the knee in order to keep socks and stockings in place.

see Accessories 18, Elastic 100

A glove that covers the wrist, hand, fingers and forearms to provide covering and protection. Gauntlets may be produced from a wide variety of materials, including leather and steel. Gauntlets were a fundamental part of a protective suit of armour to protect the hands. Nowadays, gloves with one opening for all the fingers are sometimes called gauntlets. Pictured is a white leather female riding gauntlet decorated with lace and a tapestry woven in silk and gold, possibly created by Sheldon Tapestry Workshops in the 16th or 17th century.

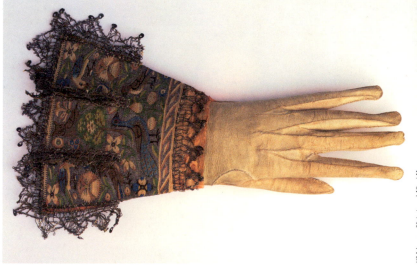

V&A Images/Victoria and Albert Museum

☞ see Elizabethan 101

A female Japanese entertainer or artist noted for wearing the traditional kimono. Geisha is a composite of two Kanji characters, *gei*, meaning performing arts and *sha*, meaning person or doer. Geisha are skilled in music, singing, dancing and pleasant conversation.

☞ see Costume 78, Kimono 146

Designs based on simple shapes such as the circle, square, triangle and trapezoid. This Yves Saint Laurent dress carries a geometric design appropriated from the work of Piet Mondrian.

A lightweight cotton cloth, usually checked. Gingham typically combines white with red, blue or green and is often used for test work due to its cheapness. Pictured in this 1965 photograph by John French, published in UK newspaper *The Daily Mail*, are various mix 'n' match gingham outfits modelled by Marie-Lise Gres, Moyra Swann and Paulene Stone. The stark contrast of black and white inherent in gingham was typical of the mod style of the mid-1960s.

V&A Images/Victoria and Albert Museum

☞ see Fabric 107

Zoe Irvin

Music-related fashion from the early and mid-1970s with colourful ambisexual outfits, such as platform shoes and single-piece glitter suits with flared trousers in satin and silk.

☞ see Heels 130

Scaling a garment or shoe pattern to a different size by increasing or decreasing important points of it. A size 10 dress pattern can be graded to produce patterns for sizes 12, 14, 16 and so on. The following table shows standard women's dress sizes in different countries:

US	UK	Euro
6	8	34
8	10	36
10	12	38
12	14	40
14	16	42
16	18	44
18	20	46
20	22	48

The alignment of fibres in a textile giving it a certain appearance and texture. A simple woven fabric has a grain that runs in two directions, with the warp and weft having equal weight. Evidence of the grain can easily be seen by tearing a piece of cotton: it forms a triangular hole as the tear extends equally along both the warp and weft. Different weaving methods produce different grains, such as twill, which produces diagonal ribs.

Direction
A piece of fabric typically has a right and wrong side due to the way the warp and weft are combined.

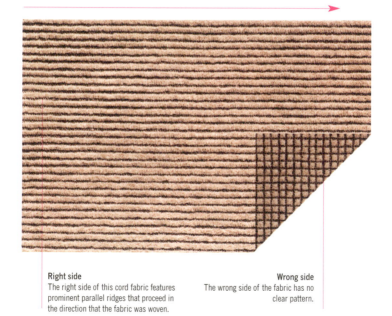

Right side
The right side of this cord fabric features prominent parallel ridges that proceed in the direction that the fabric was woven.

Wrong side
The wrong side of the fabric has no clear pattern.

see Warp & Weft 264

Kenny Yeoh

A top for women with a single, sometimes tied strap that passes behind the back of the neck. Halter-neck garments typically leave the back exposed.

Crown
The part covering the top of the head.

Brim
A broad, circular rim that juts out stiffly
from the base of the hat's crown.

Hatband
A strip of material at
the junction of the crown
and brim, holding the
hat's size.

Sweatband
The inside part of the hat
that touches the head of
the wearer.

A piece of clothing worn on the head, with a high crown and brim.

Bowler
A hard, felt hat with rounded crown to offer protection while riding. The bowler was created for Thomas Coke, second earl of Leicester, in 1850 by James and George Lock and was named after a prototype produced by Thomas and William Bowler.

Homburg
A stiff, felt hat with a crease or centre dent from front to back of the crown, but with no pinches and a sharply turned up brim all the way around. The homburg was popularised by Edward VII of England after he visited Germany.

Stetson
A wide-brimmed hat with tall crown produced in the 19th century by the John B. Stetson Company in Missouri, USA. It provides both sun and rain protection.

Slouch
A wide-brimmed, felt hat with chinstrap of British origin, commonly used by the Australian army.

see Deerstalker 89, Fedora 110, Fez 112, Helmet 131, Top Hat 246

Exclusive custom-fitted fashions that are the pinnacle of the fashion industry. Haute couture, which is French for high sewing or dressmaking, has become a global industry that drives clothing retail and a significant part of magazine sales. Haute couture garments are made to measure and are typically produced from high-quality materials, which are sewn with extreme attention to detail and finish, often by hand. Haute couture originated in 18th-century France when fashions of the court at Versailles were imitated across Europe. The modern industry was begun by Charles Frederick Worth (1826–1895), who created one-of-a-kind designs and prepared designs shown on live models. Pictured is an evening dress created by French designer Coco Chanel in the late 20th century.

V&A Images/Victoria and Albert Museum

An element called a top piece that is added to the rear end of the sole of a shoe, lifting the back of the shoe away from the ground. The heel may be made of wood covered with leather or another material presented in a range of styles. Pictured is a pair of platform shoes (1993) in bright blue leather stamped with an animal skin pattern, designed by Vivienne Westwood.

Kitten A low-height heel tapering to a point that is set forward.

Stiletto A high, tapered, narrow heel, often containing a metal rod similar to a stiletto knife, after which it is named.

Court A medium- to high-block heel.

Cuban A broad, medium-height heel that has a slightly tapered back and straight front often used with boots.

Wedge A broad, wedge-shaped heel that is an extension of the shoe sole.

Platform A high and broad heel that is accompanied by a similar sole.

V&A Images/Victoria and Albert Museum

Protective headgear used in the military, as well as construction, mining, sports, motorcycling and other activities. Helmets offer a varying degree of protection according to the amount of the head they cover – from the shallow plate helmets used by British soldiers during the First World War, covering just the top of the head, to full-face helmets used by motorcyclists. Traditional metal helmet construction materials have now been replaced by lightweight compounds, such as Kevlar-reinforced plastic composites and fillers, such as polystyrene. Pictured is a 1960s' white fur helmet from the collection at London's V&A Museum, which provides a fashion interpretation to subvert our normal conception of this item.

The edge of a piece of cloth or garment folded up and sewn down in order to enclose the cut edge so that it cannot unravel. Hems can be hem stitched or blind stitched (which will not leave a visible line of stitches), or can be stitched with a sewing machine (which does leave a visible line of stitches). Haute couture hems tend to be sewn by hand to have invisible hem stitching. A dressmaker's hem of loose running stitch is often added to heavy material so that the cloth weight does not hang from one line of stitches.

☞ see Garment 118, Stitches 225

V&A Images/Victoria and Albert Museum

A subculture or counterculture from the 1960s and 1970s with an emphasis on civil rights, sexual liberation and a peaceful anti-war and anti-nuclear stance. The hippy culture later morphed into the psychedelic subculture, which was known for its use of recreational drugs for spiritual, artistic and hedonistic ends. The hippy culture has had a lasting influence on fashion and is periodically reprised through vibrantly-coloured, often ethnic, flowing fabrics with frills, beading and crochet, such as the crocheted waistcoat by Birgitta Bjork and synthetic satin blouse by Ossie Clark shown in this image from the V&A Museum collection.

☞ see Crochet 81, Subcultures 228

Tight-fitting knitted garments worn on the feet and legs. Hosiery is made in various designs and mesh configurations with stretching fabrics, such as nylon and Lycra, which help it to mould to the body form. Formerly, hosiery made from wool and silk were worn with garters or suspender belts to stop them falling down. The name hosiery comes from *hose*, Middle English for stocking.

☞ **see Garter 119, Natural Fibres 175**

Aaron Twa

A duotone textile pattern of checks or four-pointed shapes, used particularly for outerwear, jackets and skirts. Houndstooth or dog-tooth check first appeared in the 1930s. Photographed by John French, this image shows Grace Coddington wearing a houndstooth coat by Nina Ricci.

see Pattern (fabric) 182

Artwork that explains, exemplifies or adorns.
Illustration, whether by hand or digital, allows a designer
to quickly articulate ideas and generate design concepts
in a visual form.

☞ see Concept 74, Sketch & Sketchbook 221

Exit_Nume

V&A Images/Victoria and Albert Museum

A technological, socio-economic and cultural revolution that began in 18th-century England and saw mechanisation replace manual labour. The textile and wool industries were the first to benefit with increased production capacity, prompting people to flood into growing cities like Manchester from the country. Industrialisation replaced the spinning wheel and hand loom and saw improvements in raw material production. The subsequent growth of the weaving industry saw manufactured cotton goods become the dominant British export. Pictured is an 1835 illustration of mule spinning drawn by T. Allom and engraved by J.W. Lowry from *History of the Cotton Manufacture* by Sir Edward Baines.

The source of creative ideas, inspiration, can come from many different direct and indirect sources. These can include fashions worn in other periods of history, the natural or architectural environment, science, materials, philosophy, or just about anything. Inspiration is often required in order for designers to add new twists and juxtapositions to already familiar garments. The image on the right shows an ensemble created by Vivienne Westwood (1980), which may have been inspired by the pirates of the 17th and 18th centuries (above).

V&A Images/Victoria and Albert Museum

☞ see Collection 71, Ensemble 103, Garment 118, Juxtaposition 144

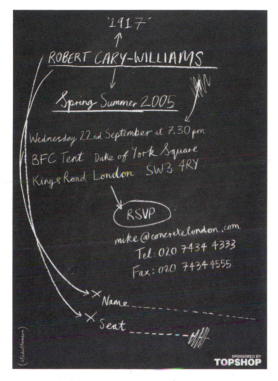

A printed card or other substrate that requests the presence of the recipient to attend a particular event. Invites are mailed to people, inviting them to attend a wide range of events in the fashion industry, including new collection shows, store openings, product launches and receptions. Pictured is an invite for the spring/summer 2005 collection of Robert-Cary Williams, created by Studio Thomson for UK clothing retailer Topshop.

A thigh- or waist-length coat that may be fastened with buttons, a zip, press studs or toggles. Jackets have full-length arms and tend to have pockets on the front or sides. Jacket styles include blazer, donkey jacket, flight or bomber jacket, Harrington jacket, jeans jacket, leather jacket, snorkel or parka and windbreaker. Pictured is a black silk and yellow sequinned jacket from the late 20th century by Karl Lagerfeld for fashion house Chanel.

V&A Images/Victoria and Albert Museum

☞ see Coat 68

A versatile weaving method that allows a warp thread to be raised independently of the other warp threads, thus allowing the production of an unlimited variety of woven patterns. Jacquard weaving was invented by Joseph-Marie Jacquard (1752–1834). Early Jacquard looms used patterns punched into cards in order to produce patterned fabric, but modern electronic looms can now control over 10,000 warp ends, providing great diversity and obviating the need to use repeat patterns. Loom preparation time makes Jacquard-produced cloth more expensive than cloth woven by simpler methods and it is used to make damask, brocade and tapestries.

Decorative objects worn on the person or clothes, often made with precious metals such as gold, silver and platinum and gemstones such as diamonds, rubies and emeralds. Jewellery includes tiaras, earrings, necklaces, rings, bracelets and other objects such as jewellery for body piercings. Jewellery was formerly a means of storing wealth and fastening clothing, but it is nowadays mainly decorative and ranges in worth from relatively valueless costume jewellery to pieces that cost millions.

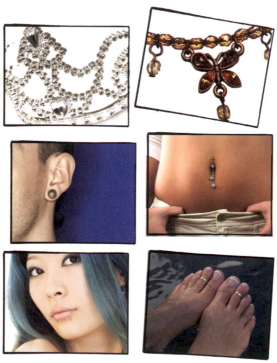

see Accessories 18, Piercing 188

Tight-fitting trousers worn for horse riding. Named after the city in India where they were originally made, they feature a tight fit on the lower legs but are flared above the knee and incorporate specialist riding adaptations, including seams on the outside of the leg, a wear patch inside the knee and a harder-wear seat panel. The use of modern stretch fabrics saw jodhpurs adapted for fashion in the 1980s, and they were worn by New Romantic bands such as Duran Duran, Spandau Ballet, Adam and the Ants and Simple Minds.

The placement of images side by side to highlight or create a relationship between them. Taken from the Latin, *juxta*, meaning near, juxtaposing different items or elements is often used as a means of generating ideas in the creative process. For example, what results do we get from combining Victoriana with tartan, or a dandy with leather?

☞ see Dandy 86, Leather 151, Tartan 236–237, Victoriana 260

A one-piece garment from Scotland made from tartan or plaid cloth. A kilt wraps around the wearer, extending from the waist to just above the knees and is fastened with straps and buckles on both ends. A kilt is traditionally worn with a belt, jacket, sporran (a type of pouch) and a dirk or dagger, but not with underwear.

☞ see Costume 78, Garment 118, Plaid 193, Tartan 236–237

A traditional Japanese garment. Literally, *kimono* means something worn and once referred to any item of clothing. Now it commonly describes a full-length, T-shaped robe, with long, wide sleeves and collars. The garment is wrapped with the left side over the right and is tied at the back with a wide belt called an *obi*. Whereas the man's kimono outfit is quite simple, the choice of kimono for women can depend on age, marital status and formality of the occasion. Few people now wear a kimono on a daily basis, particularly as a woman's traditional kimono can cost in excess of £5,000/US$10,000.

Nuno Silva

A style that is considered to be overly sentimental and/or pretentious. Kitsch often draws upon mass culture and mass-produced items that may previously have been met with critical disdain. As fashions change, what was once kitsch becomes cool. While aesthetically considered bad taste or garish, many people take pleasure in kitsch designs, whether ironically or not. French designer Jean Paul Gaultier is known for injecting kitsch into the usually sophisticated world of couture.

see Fashion Cycle 108

A method for producing cloth from wool or other types of thread, in which loops or stitches are pulled through each other using two or more needles. Knitting differs from crochet in that it has multiple active stitches held on a needle until they are ready to be used in the knitting sequence. Knitting can use a range of different yarns and needles of various gauges to produce garments with different finishes and textures, some of which are shown below.

Plain jersey knit
A single knit that stretches more in width than length.

Purl knit
A stitch that stretches the same amount in both directions.

Rib knit
A single knit used for cuffs and waistbands designed to stretch in the cross-wise direction without losing shape.

Cable knit
A method that sees stitches knitted in different orders by passing some stitches to a cable needle while other stitches are knitted, before knitting the passed stitches.

☞ see Crochet 81, Wool 267, Yarn 269

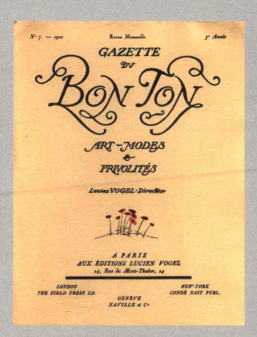

A leading European fashion magazine published in the 1910s and 1920s and founded by Lucien Vogel in 1912. *La Gazette du Bon Ton* presented fashion, lifestyle and beauty trends with dramatic garment illustrations by many art deco artists.

see Magazine 157

The two triangular pieces of cloth that extend from the collar of a suit jacket. The lapels fold back on to the front of the jacket and leave a triangular space between them, such as that pictured here. The points of the lapels vary in length and shape and are influenced by the fashion of the day.

A material produced from the tanned hides and skins of many different animals, but usually cattle, sheep, pig and goat. There is much controversy surrounding the ethics of using leather and animal products in the fashion world. Types of leather can include:

Aniline and semi-aniline leather
Leather with little or no surface coating. These are the most natural-looking leathers but they have little protection against dirt and moisture.

Pigmented leather
The grain surface of pigmented leather has a protective effect but is less natural-looking.

Full and corrected grain leather
The surface grain of leather can be abraded to certain degrees to create different leather types.

Pull-up leather
Leather that has been stretched to lighten the colour and create a worn-in effect.

Suede
The grain surface of suede is slightly abraded and buffed to create a soft, velvety texture.

Buckskin
The surface is tanned using fatty animal materials to create a supple, smooth material.

The various divisions of a garment that are used to describe its shape or appearance. These lines include the neckline, hemline, trouser length, shoulder and waistlines. Straight lines are typically thought of as hard and masculine, while curved lines are viewed as softer and more feminine. Pictured is a model wearing a dress that has a low-cut neckline, a waistline that sits on the hips and a short hemline. The various lines are softened by the delicate fabric, creating a feminine look.

Gordana Sermek

☞ see Bias 36, Neck 176, Silhouette 220, Skirt Length 222

A variety of garments used by women as underwear, made from materials such as silk, cotton, satin, polyester and nylon. Lingerie derives from *linge*, French for linen. Lingerie can be a single piece that drapes, such as a babydoll or négligée, or that has a tighter fit, such as a basque, corset, bustier or body-stocking. Upper garments include a camisole, chemise, brassiere and corselette. These are typically worn with shorts or knickers, such as boy shorts, cami shorts, French knickers, g-strings or thongs. Other lingerie items include the suspender belt, garters, stockings and tights.

Babydoll
A short nightgown or négligée used for nightwear.

Basque
A tight, form-fitting bodice or coat.

Boy shorts
Knickers that resemble male shorts.

Camisole
A sleeveless and tight-fitting top.

Corset
A bodice that moulds and shapes the torso.

Corselette
A brassiere with a girdle.

G-string
A narrow garment that passes between the buttocks and is attached to a band around the hips.

 see Baby Doll 26, Basque 33, Bra 52, Thong 242

A graphic symbol designed to represent the character of a company, product, service or other entity. Logos are ubiquitous in the fashion industry, where they are used to differentiate similar-looking clothes produced by different designers (tennis/polo shirts, for example). Branding has now developed to the extent that clothing and accessories are purchased as much for the brand they sport as the characteristics and appearance of the item.

FRED PERRY

Paul Smith

Lacoste, the clothing label founded by French tennis champion Henri Lacoste in 1933, produced tennis shirts with a crocodile appliqué embroidered on the chest, the first externally branded clothing.

The laurel logo of the Fred Perry brand, based on the old Wimbledon symbol, was the first brand to be stitched, rather than ironed, on to the garment fabric.

Paul Smith's logo, made to look like a signature, conveys the idea of a personal guarantee of bespoke quality.

TOMMY ▬ HILFIGER

Sporting the red, white and blue colours of the US flag, Tommy is one of the most successful fashion logos, appearing on a vast range of merchandise conveying American simplicity.

Featuring a Medusa head from Greek mythology, the Versace logo alludes to a classical world that all people understand, while highlighting a measure of class and wealth.

Created in 1971 by Carolyn Davidson, the Nike Swoosh, with its wing-like shape, graphically conveys rapid movement and helped propel the company to become one of the biggest sports apparel manufacturers. Nike is named after the Greek goddess of victory.

☞ **see Brand 51**

A publication featuring styles and conceptual creative ideas, influences and inspirations. Pictured is a look book for Kronk, by Parent Design. Fashion designers might use look books to demonstrate the theme and concept of a seaonal collection.

see Concept 74, Season 213, Theme 241

Germany Feng

A waterproof raincoat made from a fabric invented in 1823 by Scottish chemist Charles Macintosh. Macintosh discovered waterproof fabric while analysing the waste products of gasworks. He used rubber dissolved in coal-tar naphtha to cement two pieces of cloth together and found that the material he had created could not be penetrated by water.

☞ see Coat 68

A printed or Web-based periodical containing articles of general interest, financed by paid advertising, subscription, retail sales or a combination thereof and published at regular intervals. Magazines are one of the cornerstones of the fashion industry, using lush images of designs and collections printed four-colour on quality stock. The most influential fashion magazine is *Vogue*. First published in 1892, it gained prominence following its 1909 purchase by publisher Condé Nast and under the editorship of Edna Woolman Chase (1914–1951). Pictured is *Tank*, an independent fashion, art and architecture magazine launched in 1998 that makes great use of experimental design.

☞ see Advertising 19, La Gazette du Bon Ton 149

Fibres for producing fabric made from petro-based materials or cellulose biopolymers. Biopolymers include cellulose acetate or acetate rayon, first produced in 1924 from cotton or tree pulp cellulose. Rayon has similar properties to natural fibres like silk, wool, cotton and linen, and is soft, smooth, cool, comfortable, easily dyed and highly absorbent, but has low elastic recovery, low durability and appearance retention. Lyocell fibre is made from wood pulp cellulose, first produced in 1988. It is also a type of rayon and is resistant to wrinkles and able to simulate textures such as suede, leather, or silk. Early biopolymers were replaced by cheaper petro-based fibres, such as nylon and polyester. Nylon was first produced in 1935 as a replacement for Asian silk for parachutes and has since been used for a wide range of clothing purposes. Polyester is a cotton replacement and is the most widely used manufactured fibre in the USA. Spandex or elastane is a synthetic fibre known for its exceptional elasticity. First produced in 1959, spandex has become a mainstay for contour-hugging sports clothing, such as the Lycra bra top pictured.

Philip Date

see Elastic 100, Natural Fibres 175, Protein Fabrics 199

Andrey Armyagov

A life-size doll with human form and articulated joints used to display clothing. Fashion mannequins originated with the increased use of plate-glass windows in retail outlets in the 1880s. Mannequins became popular in the 1930s following the creation (by soap sculptor Lester Gaba) of mannequins with realistic facial features. They were mass produced with the advent of fibreglass and plastic from the 1960s onwards. Mannequins are not to be confused with a tailor's dummy, used in dressmaking and tailoring.

☞ see Dummy 97

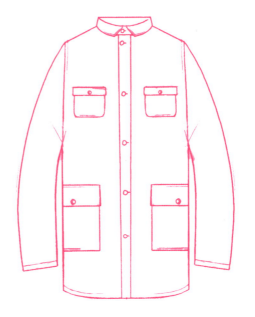

Anthony Fourrier

The Zhongshan suit, introduced by Mao Zedong as China's national dress after the founding of the Republic of China in 1950. The Mao suit caters to Western sensibilities while maintaining a Chinese character – the various elements are said to represent the most important of Communist China's ideals and values. Adopted by the Chinese Communist Party, it became a symbol of proletarian unity, though it has been abandoned by the current generation.

 see Collar 70

S Duffett

A flat female shoe with rounded, closed toes and a
buckled strap across the instep, named after a character
created by the Brown Shoe Company. Modern variations
include platform soles and chunky heels. The shoes are
often complemented with knee-high socks or tights in
dark colours or patterns, as pictured.

see Shoes 218

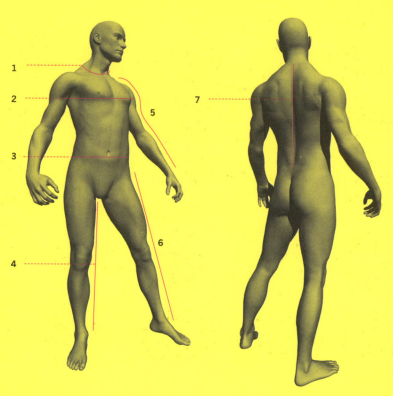

1 Collar   **2** Chest   **3** Waist   **4** Inside Leg   **5** Sleeve   **6** Outside Leg   **7** Centre Back Length

The **collar** is measured around the neck base where a shirt fits. The **chest** is a measure around the fullest part with the tape held close under the arms to ensure it is high up at the back and over the shoulder blades. The **waist** is measured around the natural waistline over any under garments that may be worn. The **inside leg** is measured from the top of the leg at the crotch to the base of the shin or hemline. The **sleeve** is measured from the neck point – where the collar seam is on the shoulder line – along the shoulder and down the outer sleeve to the cut edge. The **outside leg** is measured from the natural waistline to the bottom of the shin, and the **centre back length** is from the centre of the neck at the collar seam to the waist.

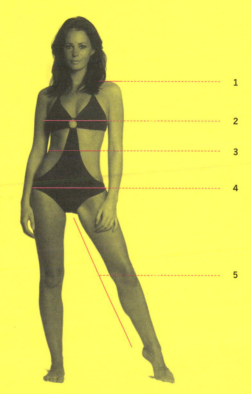

1 Neck   2 Bust   3 Waist   4 Hips   5 Inside leg or inseam

The **neck** is measured around the largest part of neck. The **bust** is measured under the arms and around the fullest part of the chest. The natural **waistline** can be found by tying a string snugly around the waist and then reaching down the side of each leg. The string will ride to the natural waist where it can be measured. **Hip** size is a measure of the fullest part of the low hip. The **inside leg** or **inseam** is a measurement from the crotch to the ankle on the inside of the leg. This can be measured by holding a ruler between the legs at the crotch and measuring from the ankle to this.

Designers create their designs using various different media according to their ability to impart colour and texture, for speed of use, but above all due to personal preference.

Marker pen
Pens with their own ink-source and a porous tip that may be permanent or non-permanent. Quick, easy to use and rapid drying.

Watercolour pencils
Typically a wooden sheath containing a range of solid pigment strips that produce coloured marks. Quick and easy to use, watercolour pencils allow a degree of colour mixing on the paper.

Pastel
A stick of pure powdered pigment and binder. Pastels are quick and easy to use, and allow colour mixing on the paper. However, they can be messy and designs need to be fixed after completion to avoid smudging.

Gouache
Brush- or blade-applied paint consisting of pigment suspended in water with white pigment. Gouache is more opaque and has more intense hues than watercolour paint and requires drying time.

Acrylic paint
A brush- or blade-applied fast-drying paint containing pigment suspended in an acrylic polymer emulsion. Water resistant, acrylic paint can be thinned with water and made into washes and does not require solvent use.

Watercolour paint
Brush-applied paint with finely ground pigment suspended or dissolved in water. Watercolour or watermedia gives a soft, translucent, quick-drying colour that allows show-through.

Zoe Irvin

A very short skirt that barely covers the buttocks. The micro-skirt was developed in the late 1960s following the evolution of the miniskirt.

PhotoCreate

Garments that are styled or coloured like military uniforms. Militaria in fashion includes the adaptation of camouflage patterns such as those pictured, in addition to the use of particular garments, such as combat-style boots, bomber jackets and cargo pants.

Pekka Jaakkola

Mosista Pambudi

The craft of making hats and hat trim. Millinery refers to the hats designed, produced and sold by a milliner and probably derives from the Middle English *milener*, which means native of the Italian city Milan – a source of bonnets, lace and other hat-making materials. Millinery provided the starting ground for many famous designers, including Coco Chanel.

☞ see Hats 128

The movement that has led to fashion designs that are stripped down to the most fundamental and expressive features. Minimalism developed in fashion following the Second World War and applies the principles of methodological reductionism seen in Ockram's Razor – a principle that states that elements that are not really needed should be pared back to produce something simpler, thus reducing the risk of introducing inconsistencies, ambiguities and redundancies. Minimalism was popular with Japanese designers such as Issey Miyake in the 1980s and 1990s.

Zoe Irvin

Mini

A short skirt with a hemline that is typically at least 20cm or eight inches above the knee. The miniskirt became popular in the 1960s and marked the high point of hemline creep that began with the flapper style of the 1920s. The development of the miniskirt is generally attributed to English designer Mary Quant. As a rule of thumb, if the wearer of a skirt cannot reach past its hemline with her ring and index finger, it is not a mini.

Maxi

By contrast, a maxi-skirt is an ankle-length skirt that was popular in the 1970s as a reaction to the miniskirt. Skirts could not get any shorter and so they got longer instead. The development of the maxi-skirt coincided with the rise of the feminist movement, which abhorred the way the miniskirt had turned women into erotic objects.

☞ see Flapper 113, Micro-skirt 165, Skirt Length 222

Anthony Fourrier

A subculture originating in London from the late 1950s to mid-1960s that developed around the jazz and rhythm-and-blues music scene. mod or modernist fashion had as its central element slim-cut Italian suits. A Mod revival in the early 1980s saw the return of close-fitting three-button suits, Fred Perry and Ben Sherman shirts, Sta-Prest trousers and Levi's 501 jeans.

☞ see Subcultures 228

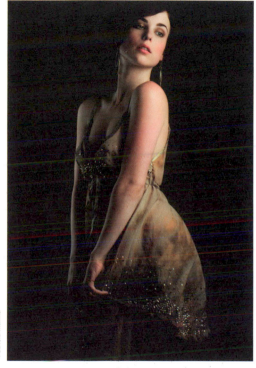

Patricia Malina

A person employed to wear clothing for its presentation at a fashion show, photo shoot or advertisement. The use of live models rather than mannequins is thought to have begun in 1853 when Parisian shop girl, Marie Vernet Worth, modelled garments for her designer husband Charles Frederick Worth. In print publications, high fashion models use their face and body to express the different emotions required in artistic constructions relating to the garments, jewels or cosmetics that are worn. Fashion models wear garments on the catwalk or runway and pose to display their outfits during a fashion show.

☞ see Magazine 157, Photography 187

A silk-like fibre made from the hair of the angora goat that is durable and resilient, that has high lustre and sheen. Mohair is sometimes used as a substitute for animal fur in the creation of fashion garments. Pictured is a woman's mohair jumper created by Vivienne Westwood and Malcolm McLaren in 1976.

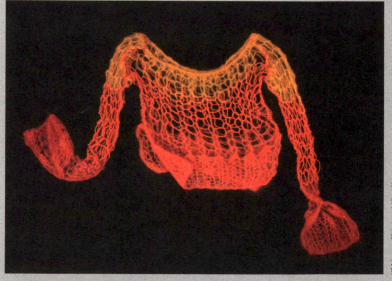

V&A Images/Victoria and Albert Museum

☞ see Natural Fibres 175

Alexander Gitlits

The use of a single colour. Monochromatic fashions are those where all the garments of an outfit share the same single colour to provide consistency and cohesiveness. Black is typically used in a monochromatic outfit, following the axiom that black is always in fashion, but white and grey are also used.

☞ see Colour Wheel 72

In shirtmaking, a measure of the back of the neck where it meets the shoulders.

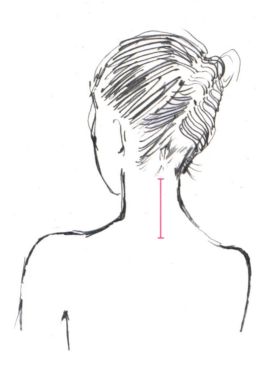

Zoe Irvin

👉 see Measurements 162–163

Fibres from plants and animals that can be spun into a thread such as wool, silk, linen, cotton and hemp.

Wool

Fibre from animal fur of the *caprinae* family, such as sheep, goats, alpacas and rabbits.

Cotton

A fibre that grows around the seeds of the cotton plant *Gossypium* species that is spun into thread and is the most widely-used natural fibre. Cotton is strong, durable and absorbent.

Silk

A fibre obtained from the cocoons made by *Bombyx Mori* silkworm larvae, prized for its shimmering appearance due to the fibres' prism-like structures that refract light.

Linen

A fibre made from flax *Linum Usitatissimum*, linen is the world's oldest textile material and is frequently used for towels, sheets and tablecloths, in addition to shirts and other garments.

☞ see Alpaca 20, Man-made Fibres 158, Protein Fabrics 199

Anthony Fournier

The part of an upper body garment that circles the neck of the wearer. Garment necks are finished in many different ways and styles, they may be open or closed, and may have different fastenings, such as zips, buttons, poppers, buckles and velcro.

A-neck The neck of a standard shirt that buttons at the throat and whose collar folds back and down to give a shape like a majuscule A.

Ballerina A low neckline typical of a strapless or spaghetti-strap dress.

Bateau/boat A high and wide neckline that runs straight across the front and back and meets at the shoulders.

Crew A close-fitting, ribbed round neck.

Diamond A diamond-shaped cutout that fastens at the front or back neckline.

Jewel A high and round neckline that rests at the neck base.

Keyhole A tear-shaped or round cutout that fastens at the front or back neckline.

Off-the-shoulder A wide neck that leaves the shoulders bare or covered with a sheer yoke of net or organza attached to a high collar.

Polo A sweater or jersey with a high, close-fitting collar.

Scoop neck A u-shaped neck that falls towards the bust, often showing significant cleavage.

Split A round neck cut with a small V in the centre.

Square An open-yoke neckline shaped like half a square.

Turtle A high, close-fitting, turnover collar used for sweaters.

V-neck An open yoke forming a V shape in the bodice.

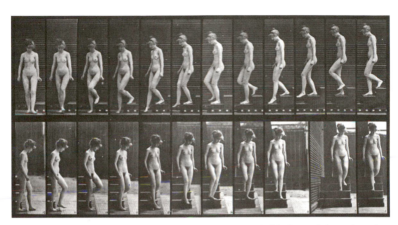

Anton Oparin

Above: 'Woman Walking Downstairs', a motion study by Victorian photographer Eadweard Muybridge.

Far left: Typical dress of the late Victorian era.

Left: A stark contrast to Victorian fashions, contemporary clothes are often much more revealing through the use of low cuts and sheer materials.

Nudity can be full or partial, but generally refers to occasions when a person wears fewer clothes than is typically socially acceptable and exposes bare skin. Social perceptions are one of the defining elements of the acceptability of partial nudity and they change as the overriding zeitgeist changes. Fashion often willingly challenges and steps over the line of what is considered acceptable, as has been seen with the development of garments such as the bikini and miniskirt. A more recent example is the midriff-revealing crop or 'muffin' top.

☞ see Bikini 37, Peek-a-boo 185, Sheer 217

A strong, lightweight material with elastic properties used for clothing and other items. Nylon was the first man-made fibre, developed by DuPont in the early 1930s. It is noted for its bright lustre, sheerness, abrasion resistance, ease of washing and drying, and colour resistance. It is commonly known for its use in women's stockings during the 1940s. Chemists from New York and London were originally responsible for developing the compound material, hence the popular theory that 'Nylon' stands for New York–London. However, DuPont first claimed 'nyl' was randomly chosen, while 'on' was copied from the suffixes of other fibres such as 'rayon' and 'cotton'.

Aaron Twa

☞ see Hosiery 134, Man-made Fibres 158

A brimmed hat originating in Cuenca, Ecuador, from the plaited leaves of the panama-hat palm *Carludovica palmata*. Panamas obtained widespread popularity after President Roosevelt wore one when he visited the Panama Canal. Pictured are Panamas in a factory in rural Ecuador.

☞ see Hats 128

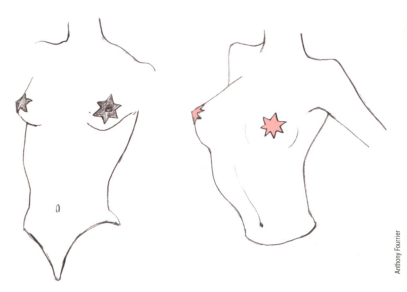

Anthony Fourrier

Coverings for the nipples, applied with glue or a self-adhesive backing, and used in place of a bra or bikini top when a woman is topless or wearing transparent clothing. Pasties provide no support and only provide minimal visual breast coverage, so are used mainly when showing the nipple is forbidden, or for decorative purposes. Pasties can be decorated in many ways, from flower or heart shapes to tassels and sequins. Pasties grew in popularity in the 1920s and are often worn by strippers/dancers at venues such as the Folies Bergere in Paris, France. In the 1960s, designers combined pasties and briefs and created the trikini.

📌 see Burlesque 58, Lingerie 153

Anthony Fournier

A piece of fabric that is used to cover part of a garment.
Patches may be sewn over the parts of clothing that
cover the knees or elbows to provide additional wear
resistance or to repair wear damage. Colourful patches
are also added for communicative and decorative
purposes, such as the insignia on military
and police uniforms.

☞ see Epaulette 104, Uniform 256

A repeated decorative design that can be printed, stitched or woven into a fabric. The popularity of certain patterns often undergoes as much change as the garments themselves.

Paisley
A droplet-shaped motif of Persian origin, also called Persian pickles.

Polka dot
A pattern consisting of dots, which became popular in late 19th-century Britain.

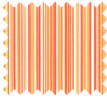

Stripes
Long, straight bands of single colours running vertically.

Hoops
Long, straight bands of single colours running horizontally.

Plaid
A cross-hatched dyeing pattern used for wool clothing.

Tie dye
A brightly coloured pattern produced by tying fabric before applying dye so it only reaches certain areas.

Houndstooth or dog-tooth
A rich, textural, duotone pattern of abstracted angular shapes that first appeared in the 1930s.

Harlequin
A lozenge or diamond pattern typically worn by the comic character in dramatic works.

Animal print
A print that resembles the pattern of animal fur such as leopard.

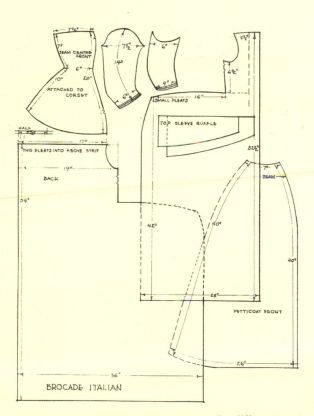

A form, template or guide used to cut out the different parts
that comprise a garment. A pattern contains the style and detail
of a garment and is made from a block, which relates to the
measurements of the body.

☞   see Block 39

V&A Images/Victoria and Albert Museum

A movement in men's clothing in the 1960s featuring bright colours, slim-fitting trousers and boots. The Peacock Revolution was part of what made London, England, the capital of the 'swinging sixties' as tailored, plain and dark suits were left in the closet to be replaced by the brighter creations such as the Tommy Nutter suit (1969) pictured. Frills and cravats re-emerged as unisex fashion and sporting vivid shirt prints became increasingly popular.

☞ see Suit 229, Tailoring 232

Alexander Gitlits

Any part of the garment that has been cut out to reveal skin or underwear such as this dress, which reveals the flank. Often used to make underwear more revealing.

☞ see Nudity 177, Sheer 217

An undergarment worn by women under a skirt, dress or sari. Petticoats hang from the waist or shoulders and are worn for warmth, to give shape to the overlaying skirt or to prevent a skirt or dress from clinging to the wearer's body. Petticoats evolved alongside the outer garments they were worn with, such as the beautiful lace petticoats that were developed to be worn with silk dresses in the 18th century. Petticoats have been in and out of fashion as skirts have oscillated between wide and narrow. Following a revival in the 1950s led by Christian Dior, petticoats have fallen into one of their periods of disuse although they are still used for practical purposes and they sometimes appear in alternative subculture trends.

see Victoriana 260

The process of making pictures by recording light on a light-sensitive film or sensor. Photography is used by the fashion industry to present images of garments for promotional purposes. The resulting images often present conceptual attitudes and narratives intended to convey certain attributes to the collection or garment, particularly in images taken for magazines such as those presented here.

☞ see Art Direction 24, Collection 71, Magazine 157

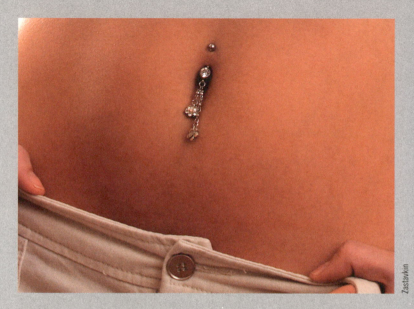

Zastavkin

A form of body modification that sees the insertion of a piece of jewellery into an opening punctured, pierced or cut into the skin for spiritual, ornamental or sexual reasons. Ear piercing has been practised continuously since ancient times by both men and women, while Indian women have practised nostril piercing for centuries. In modern times, piercing in the West was adopted by hippy men in the 1960s and the 1970s punk subculture. Unorthodox piercings such as nipples, tongues and the face began to increase in popularity with the bondage and sadomasochism subculture of the 1970s and more recently, in the last decade, lip, bellybutton and eyebrow piercings have become relatively common among teenagers and young adults as a means of fashionable self-expression.

see Cyber 84, Hippy 133, Jewellery 142, Punk 201

A woven cloth in which the warp forms loops, having been woven over a metal rod or wire. The pile ends may be left as loops to form loop pile or be cut to form cut pile such as velvet or flannel. Pile is sometimes called nap, which refers to the lay or grain of the fabric as all the fibres lay in the same direction. Garment costs using pile material may be more expensive. This is because more material is needed – sections must be cut so that the nap runs in the same direction when the pieces are sewn together. The pattern block front (shown below left) and back (shown below right) run in the same direction so that when cut and constructed, the fabric grain runs in the same direction to give consistent colour and texture. Nap fabrics can also be 'shaded' as the direction that the cloth is cut affects how bright it appears. The nap of velvet feels coarse in one direction and produces a dull, matte appearance, but it appears silky smooth in the opposite direction with a bright, shiny appearance because the fibres fall together.

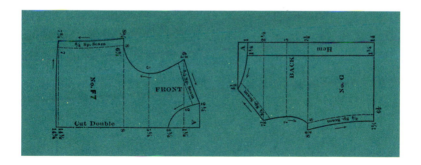

☞ see Warp & Weft 264

V&A Images/Victoria and Albert Museum

A sleeveless, collarless garment tied or buttoned at the back, originally worn as an apron. Also called a pinny, a pinafore dress was intended to be worn over a top or blouse, but the name refers to any sleeveless dress that fastens behind. The name originates from the aprons that were pinned to the front of a dress. Pictured is a pinafore dress by French designer André Courrèges (1966).

☞ see Dress 95

A pair of scissors with V-shaped teeth* along the blades, created by Louise Austin in 1893 to cut fabric with a zigzag pattern. Pinking shears are used for cutting woven cloth in order to limit the length of fraying that may occur at its unfinished edges. The expression 'pinking' probably derives from pink, the common name of the garden plant *dianthus* that has zigzag-perforated petals.

Layers of fabric that cover an opening, typically found at the neck, waist or sleeve of a garment. Plackets may contain or hide fasteners and aid in their undoing. For example, pulling on a placket will undo the poppers it covers.

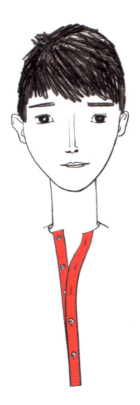

Anthony Fournier

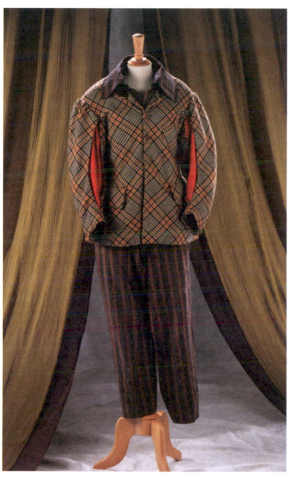

A patterned, woollen cloth with repeat horizontal and vertical blocks of colour such as tartan. Pictured is a plaid jacket with shirt and breeches in cotton and wool created by British designer Vivienne Westwood in the early 1980s.

☞ see Pattern (fabric) 182, Tartan 236–237, Wool 267

Zoe Irvin

A fold of doubled fabric that is secured in place. A pleat is normally used to reduce a wide piece of fabric to a narrower size, such as in a skirt or trousers. Pleats may be made in different ways to create different effects.

Knife pleats
These are sharp and narrow. A series of knife pleats are normally used for gathering material in a garment.

Box pleats
These consist of two parallel creases, facing in opposite directions. Box pleats give more volume to garments.

☞ **see Darts 87, Seam 212**

A bag-like container created in a garment for carrying small items such as coins. Pocket derives from Anglo-Norman French, *pocket(e)* a diminutive of *poke*, meaning pouch.

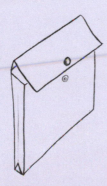
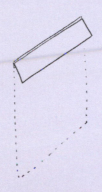
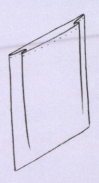

Anthony Fourrier

Cargo pocket
An expandable pocket with side pleats that may or may not have a flap, such as the button-down flap in the illustration.

Inside pocket
There are three types of inside pocket: a seam pocket that is sewn into a seam; a front hip pocket that is attached at the side waist seam; and a slashed pocket attached through a slit in the face fabric.

Patch pocket
A lined or unlined pocket normally made from the face fabric and attached directly to the fabric. This illustration features a bellows pleat.

☞ **see Jacket 140, Pleats 194**

Zoe Irvin

An outer garment comprising a single sheet of fabric with an opening for the head and perhaps the arms. Ponchos are typically associated with indigenous people of Latin America who traditionally wear brightly coloured wool ponchos.

see Wool 267

Designer clothes sold in standard sizes rather than made to measure. French for ready-to-wear, prêt-à-porter or off-the-peg clothing sacrifices the tailored fit and exquisite finish of haute couture for a lower price and ease of purchasing. Haute couture fashion houses produce prêt-à-porter ranges of their designs as the high garment turnover offers higher profits. Haute couture is French for elegant sewing and refers to the creation of exclusive fashions.

An inked design applied with pressure to fabrics such as cotton, silk or polyester. Prints are usually continuous in the horizontal and vertical planes although they can be more elaborate, as in the example pictured.

Gordana Sermek

The Dover Press

Luxurious and warm fabrics produced from natural wool or fur that are typically very soft and have a low micron diameter count. Protein fabrics include angora, mohair, cashmere, camel, alpaca and cat. Angora rabbit fur was first bred in the Carpathian Mountains to obtain cloth for warm clothing, while angora cat fur originating in Scotland in the 1890s borrowed the name. Angora goat fur is used to produce mohair. Alpaca wool is warmer and lighter than sheep's wool, with Peruvian Accoyo alpacas giving the best fibre. Cashmere is produced from the cashmere goat, while camel is cloth produced from the soft undercoat hair that is collected when camels moult in warmer seasons.

☞ see Alpaca 20, Mohair 172, Wool 267

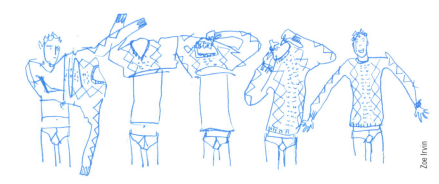

Zoe Irvin

A garment, such as a jumper or sweater, which is put on
by being pulled over the head.

☞ see Garment 118

Alexander Gitlits

An anti-establishment subculture that developed from punk rock music in the mid-1970s. Punk fashion (first developed and commercialised by Vivienne Westwood and Malcolm McLaren through their London boutique, SEX) was originally deconstructionist and anti-fashion, and was designed to be confrontational, rebellious and shocking with a disdain for established norms and niceties. Military clothing, sometimes ripped or studded, characterised punk fashion in the 1970s with cropped and sometimes dyed hair. Bands such as The Ramones, Sex Pistols and The Exploited have popularised the punk look. Punk continues to appeal to designers and has been reprised as a concept several times since the 1970s.

☞ see Deconstruction 88, Slogan 223, Subcultures 228

Bill McKelvie

Polyvinyl chloride. A tough, synthetic resin, PVC was not developed commercially until 1926 when Waldo Semon of B.F. Goodrich found a way to plasticise it. PVC has been adopted as a material of choice by fetish fashion designers due to its ability to be produced in bright, intense hues and formed into tight-fitting garments that provide a close-hugging second skin to the wearer's body form, such as the corsetry pictured here. PVC can produce a variety of sensual stimulation including tactile, visual and olfactory.

☞ see Fetish 111

European fashions in this period (late 18th–early 19th centuries), were very much influenced by the expansion of the British Empire. Women's dresses saw the introduction of the empire line – a gathering of the bulk of the dress under the breasts – and fabrics such as muslin that replaced the more expensive and heavy fabrics of previous fashions. Men's fashion too was influenced by Europe and saw jackets cut with a waist seam, high collars, top hats, riding boots and breeches, all in luxurious fabrics. Depicted is an illustration by Horace Vernet from his *Costumes d'Incroyables et Merveilleuses* (1810–1818), a series of 33 paintings that portrayed the fashionable men and women of the day.

Paris. *Incroyables.* N.14.

Culotte & Guêtres de Peau couleur de Cuir. Canne à Parapluie.

V&A Images/Victoria and Albert Museum

see Coat 68, Collar 70

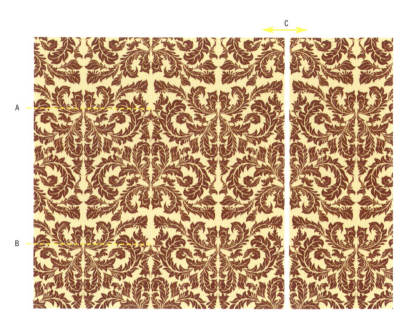

A pattern printed several times on to a fabric to cover its surface. The pattern on the print block is formed so that its bottom matches with the top of the block printed beneath it. Patterns also repeat horizontally to allow different pieces to be sewn together. In the example pictured, line A marks the top and line B the bottom of a block that is repeatedly printed on the fabric. Point C shows how two pieces of printed fabric can be joined together to form a continuous pattern.

see Block Printing 40, Pattern (fabric) 182, Print 198

A garment such as a coat that can be worn inside out. Reversible clothing allows the use of different fabric or colour combinations in the same design and gives the wearer the ability to wear a garment in different ways. In the illustration, the jacket can be worn as either orange or brown.

Archana Bhartia

A knit pattern that produces vertical stripes of
stockinette stitch alternating with vertical stripes of
reverse stockinette stitch. Ribbing is a popular finish for
hems and other edges that need to be form fitting.

A thin band of cloth that is tied to or sewn on to a garment for decoration or to act as a fastening. Ribbon is commonly made of silk, satin, lace, velvet or synthetic material.

A style originating in the music created by Elvis Presley in the 1950s that was the forerunner to rock 'n' roll. Rockabilly fashion developed around Elvis's love of denim jeans and jacket and this developed into the greaser look, characterised by long sideburns, greased back hair, tight jeans or black slacks, brothel creeper shoes, motorcycle jackets and tattoos. In Britain, rockabilly fans were called Teddy boys due to the long, Edwardian-style frock coats they wore with tight black drainpipe trousers and brothel creeper shoes.

☞ see Drainpipe 93, Edwardian 99, Tattoo 238

V&A Images/Victoria and Albert Museum

An interchangeable starched fabric frill worn at the neck of a shirt in Elizabethan England and 16th-century Europe. Pictured is a portrait of Dudley North, third Baron North (c.1589–1666) wearing an elaborate pleated ruff from the collection at London's V&A Museum.

A hard-wearing suit of a long, square-cut jacket and long or short trousers made from khaki cotton, made popular in the 19th century by Europeans visiting the African bush. Safari comes from Kiswahili, from the Arabic *safara*, meaning to travel. Pictured is a modern take on the safari suit, created by Yves Saint Laurent in the late 20th century.

V&A Images/Victoria and Albert Museum

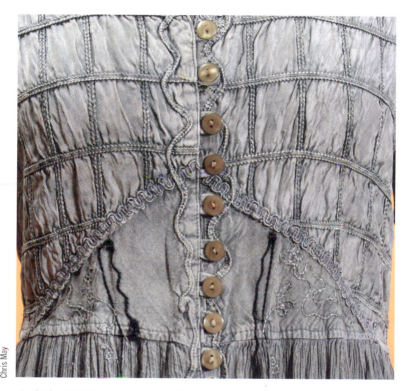

Chris May

A cloth, usually woven from silk, which has a lustrous top surface and a dull back due to the high number of 'floats' or missed interlacings where the warp thread lies over the weft thread, or vice versa. Satin is used for clothing such as evening gowns, lingerie, sports clothing and other items, such as ballet shoes. Fabric produced in this way from other thread such as cotton is called sateen.

The join line formed when two pieces of cloth are sewn together. Seams may be formed in different ways to produce different visual effects that have different levels of prominence. The 'seam allowance' is the area between the edge and the stitching line on the pieces of material being stitched together, which ranges from $1/4$ inch for curved areas to several inches for places requiring extra fabric for final fitting to the wearer.

Running seam
Two pieces of fabric are joined together using a flat bed machine. These are commonly found inside a denim jacket. Pictured is a running seam with overlocked edging.

French seam
The first stitch is applied to the right side of the fabric with the second on the wrong side to trap it. This method originated in Paris, France and is used on fine or transparent materials. Pictured is a French seam and pin hem.

Welt seam
An extremely strong bond between two pieces of fabric that are effectively interlocked together, giving a distinctive pattern. One fabric has two rows of stitching and the other only one, as commonly used with denim. Pictured is a welt seam in conjunction with top stitching.

A time period that corresponds to the seasons of the year for which designers produce specific garment collections. Fashion houses tend to produce and launch a different collection twice a year. The ideas and styles they present can loosely be termed 'this season's fashion'. The cycle takes about a year with the process to create a spring/summer collection starting in January and ending the following January with delivery into store. The autumn/winter collections start with shows in August and fulfillment into stores the following July.

fabric shows

Yarn and fabric shows start the design process with a display of the new colours and materials that are available.

delivery

Fulfilment of garment order into store, and the cycle starts again.

sampling

Samples of designs are shown to fashion buyers.

ordering

Stores order garments

The uncut edge of a woven fabric that is on the right- and left-hand edge during manufacture. Selvage or selvedge will not fray as the yarn returns on itself and thus appears finished. Selvage tends to be cut away or hidden by a hem as it may carry a different pattern to the rest of the fabric, have a different weave pattern, or lack pile.

A loop of metal or other material on the reverse of a
button that provides a means of sewing them to the
fabric, in addition to creating space under the button for
the fabric that is buttoned to sit.

Anette Linnea Rasmussen

see Button 60

Various outlines or profiles that characterise the body form. The fashion of a given time may emphasise or create a particular shape.

Pear-shaped
A figure that tapers towards the top and is rounded at the bottom. Often said of women who have wide hips and a small bust.

Hourglass
A female body shape in which the hips and bust are of proportional size, but with a narrower waist. The hourglass figure, such as that of actress Marilyn Monroe, was popular in the 1950s and 1960s and can be achieved through the use of corsetry.

Wasp-waist
A very narrow, exaggerated waist that emphasises the hips and bust (similar to a wasp), obtained through the use of corsetry and popular in the 19th century.

Jeffrey Ong Guo Xiong

A semi-transparent and flimsy fabric with a very fine knit, often used to produce tights, leggings and stockings in addition to lingerie and blouses.

Insole   Tongue

Aglet*

Eyelets

Throat line

Topline

Quarter

Heel

Top piece

Vamp or upper

Welt

Toe cap

Outsole

Footwear extending to the ankle, worn to protect the feet and made in a range of styles and materials such as leather, plastic, rubber or canvas. The main elements of a shoe are the insole, the interior bottom of the shoe that sits under the foot; the outsole, the part in direct contact with the ground; the heel (the bottom rear part of a shoe); the vamp or upper that covers the foot and helps hold the shoe on to it; and the tongue, a flap that is part of the upper and sits underneath the shoelaces.

* The plastic or metal cladding on the end of shoelaces that prevents the twine from unravelling.

see Boots 49, Shoe Types 219

Shoes are available in a range of different styles that readily reflect the changing nature of fashion.

Espadrilles
A wedge shoe with a sole/heel of braided rope.

Flip-flop
A flat sandal with one or two straps between the big and second toes. Also called thongs.

Slide
An open-toed and open-back sandal with one band across the toes.

Ballet flat
A flat shoe with a round toe and thin sole.

Mary Jane
A shoe with a strap across the vamp.

Ankle strap
A sandal with an adjustable strap attached to the back of the shoe passing across the ankle.

Court
A closed-toe shoe with a medium to high heel with pointed or rounded toe.

Clog
A shoe with a wooden, often platform sole. Also called mules.

Stiletto
A court shoe with a high, spiked heel.

Zoe Irvin

The outline or contour that a garment creates when worn.

Mermaid – Figure-hugging dress with a skirt that flares below the knees.

A-line – Shaped like a majuscule letter A.

Empire line – A high-waisted dress gathered just under the bust and with a long, loose skirt.

V-line – Wide at the shoulder narrowing at the hemline.

Sheath – A slim, straight dress without a waistline.

☞ **see Line 152**

Sketch

An initial drawn image that outlines the main visual elements of a garment design. A sketch is used to present the idea of how a garment will look, but without specific tailoring details.

Sketchbook

A book containing various sketched ideas by a designer, which may form the basis of a collection. The ideas in the sketchbook can be worked up into more detailed illustrations prior to making prototype garments.

Anthony Fourrier

A skirt or dress will have a different length depending upon its function and the prevailing fashion. Typical skirt lengths include the following:

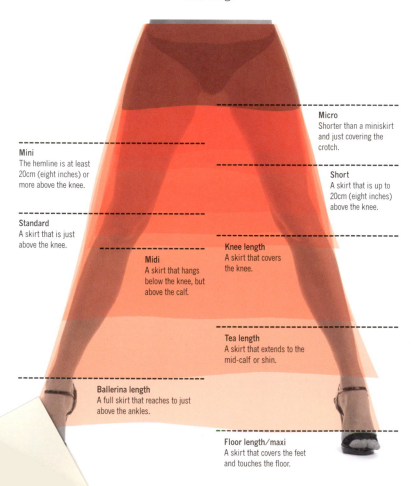

Micro
Shorter than a miniskirt and just covering the crotch.

Mini
The hemline is at least 20cm (eight inches) or more above the knee.

Short
A skirt that is up to 20cm (eight inches) above the knee.

Standard
A skirt that is just above the knee.

Midi
A skirt that hangs below the knee, but above the calf.

Knee length
A skirt that covers the knee.

Tea length
A skirt that extends to the mid-calf or shin.

Ballerina length
A full skirt that reaches to just above the ankles.

Floor length/maxi
A skirt that covers the feet and touches the floor.

Alexander Gitlits

A word or phrase, typically emblazoned across the chest of a t-shirt. Slogans on clothing originated as a visual political communication to show support for or opposition to a particular viewpoint. Appropriated by the fashion industry, slogans became endemic after designer Katherine Hamnett met former UK Prime Minister Margaret Thatcher in 1984 while wearing an anti-nuclear t-shirt (see page 285).

Zoe Irvin

A very thin shoulder strap used on garments such as camisoles, cocktail dresses and evening gowns. Named for its resemblance to spaghetti pasta.

Stitching serves various functional and decorative purposes
as these examples show.

Topstitch
A decorative row of stitching
close to the garment seam or
edge on the outer side of
the fabric to create a
strong seam.

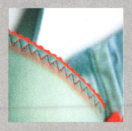

Elastic stitch
A stitch that stretches with
the fabric. Pictured is a detail
of a bra in which each
segment of the zig-zag has
three stitches, which allow
more 'give'.

Buttonhole stitch
Stitched around a buttonhole
to seal the fabric cut.

Zig-zag stitch
A stitch used for finishing to
prevent fraying.

Honeycomb stitch
A decorative stitch that
allows for fabric stretch.

Overlock stitch
Stitching that stops
fabric fraying.

☞ **see Fabric 107**

V&A Images/Victoria and Albert Museum

A band of cloth or a shawl worn around the shoulders and left to fall down the body front such as a fox-fur stole or mink. Deriving from the Latin *stola* meaning garment or equipment, it is also a Christian vestment, made from an embroidered band of silk. Pictured is a 1962 photograph by John French showing a silk evening dress trimmed with fur and matching stole designed by Nina Ricci worn by Anne Larsen.

☛ see Draping 94

Anthony Fournier

A straight band or line of differing colour to the material
on either side of it. Stripes that may be printed, sewn,
woven or knitted into the fabric. Vertical stripes can help
give an elongated appearance, making people look
thinner, while horizontal stripes or hoops often tend to
accentuate the girth of the wearer.

A group with distinct behaviours and beliefs that are different from those held by the wider culture of which they are a part. A subculture may be identified by its political or artistic views, race, sexual orientation or other values. The values of a subculture are often expressed visually by the way in which members dress and the symbols they use. Mass culture often appropriates these and assimilates them into general culture. The fashion industry recently revived visual elements from the punk subculture. Other prominent subcultures include gothic, techno and cyber.

Groups representing musical genres:
B-boy, Cyber, Disco, Emo, Goth, Grebo, Grunger, Indie, Mod, New Rave, New Romantic, Punk, Rave, Rocker, Teddy boy, Techno

Groups representing class:
Chav, Preppy, Scally, Sloane, Townie

Groups representing lifestyle/political views:
Bohemian, Gayskin, Green, Hardline, Hippy, Neo-Nazi, Skinhead

Groups representing activities/interests:
Biker, Gamer, Geek, Jock, Nerd, Otaku, Skater, Surfer

☞ see Bohemian 43, Cyber 84, Hippy 133, Punk 201

Lapel

Shoulder

Buttonhole

Breast pocket

Collar

Blade

Side vent

Centre vent

A set of clothes cut from the same fabric, designed to be worn together. A suit typically consists of a jacket and trousers or skirt, and sometimes a tie and waistcoat too. Suits can be worn for most occasions and can often say a lot about the wearer. Whether made from wool or linen, in tweed or pinstripe or with an Italian of British cut, the most important factor when choosing a suit is its tailoring and fit.

These images (left) show negotiators at the Treaty of Versailles (1919) wearing early 20th-century suits (above) and a catalogue illustrating a single-breasted and double-breasted jacket (below).

☞ see Tie 243, Waistcoat 263

A pictorial element that communicates a concept, idea or object. Symbols provide a burst of precise information, such as the garment care symbols pictured here, found on clothing labels to inform the owner about the appropriate washing method for the item.

Washing
These symbols instruct the owner as to how the garment should be washed.

Machine wash, normal (at a maximum 30 degrees Celsius)

Machine wash, normal (at a maximum 40 degrees Celsius)

Machine wash, normal (at a maximum 50 degrees Celsius)

Machine wash, normal (at a maximum 60 degrees Celsius)

Machine wash, normal (at a maximum 95 degrees Celsius)

Machine wash, extremely delicate/gentle cycle (at 30 degrees Celsius)

Machine wash, extremely delicate/gentle cycle (at a maximum temperature of 30 degrees Celsius)

Garment suitable for a cotton wash at stated temperature

Garment suitable for a woollen wash at stated temperature

Machine wash, delicate/gentle cycle (at maximum temperature of 40 degrees Celsius)

Hand wash only

Do not wash

Ironing
These symbols instruct the owner as to how the garment should be ironed.

Do not iron or press

Cool iron, 110 degrees Celsius, acrylic, nylon, acetate

Warm iron, 150 degrees Celsius, polyester mix, wool

Hot iron, 200 degrees Celsius, cotton, linen

Drying

These symbols instruct the owner as to how the garment should be dried.

Can be tumble dried

Can be tumble dried on a low setting

Can be tumble dried on a high setting

Do not tumble dry

Drip dry recommended

Hang dry

Dry flat

Dry In Shade

Bleaching

These clothing label symbols refer to whether bleach can be safely used in the garment washing process or not.

Can be chlorine bleached

Non-chlorine bleach when needed

Do not chlorine bleach

Dry cleaning

These symbols instruct the owner as to how the garment should be dry cleaned.

Dry clean

Dry clean, any solvent

Dry clean, petroleum solvent only

Do not dry clean

Dry clean, short cycle

Dry clean, reduced moisture

Dry clean, low heat

Dry clean, no steam

Bespoke menswear production in which garments such as suits are completely original and made to the measurements of the specific client. Tailoring describes the various traditional techniques used to produce a jacket.

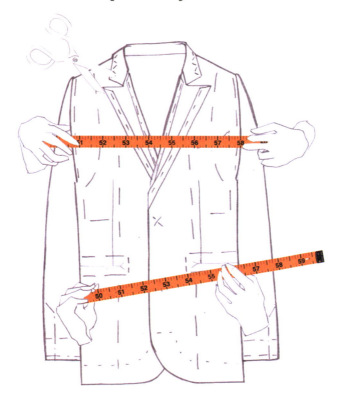

Anthony Fourrier

☞ see Suit 229

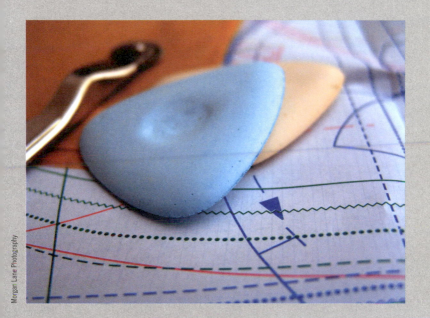

Morgan Lane Photography

A piece of hard chalk used by tailors to make temporary marks on fabric relating to the size of the client. Also known as French chalk, a tailor will chalk lines on to the cloth of a semi-made garment during a fitting in order to make precise alterations to ensure an accurate final fit.

see Tailoring 232

A sleeveless (and often brightly coloured) T-shirt worn by both men and women. The tank top takes its name from the tank suit – a one-piece women's swimsuit with shoulder straps – so named because it was worn in a swimming pool or 'tank'. A tank top, vest, or singlet in a more neutral colour is worn by men as underwear. Tank top may also refer to a sleeveless pullover or sweater.

Anthony Fourrier

☞ **see Bikini 37**

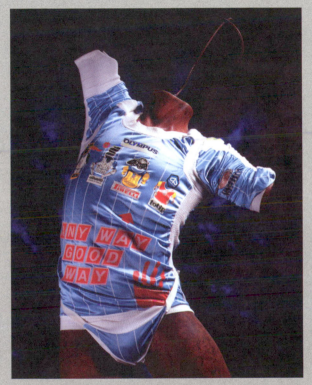

V&A Images/Victoria and Albert Museum

A skin-tight, single-piece garment covering the torso and body, but not the legs. Leotards are named after French acrobat Jules Léotard (1839–1870), the subject of the George Leybourne song *The Daring Young Man on the Flying Trapeze*. Leotards influenced the development of the swimming costume, and they allow free movement, hence their popularity among gymnasts and dancers. Pictured is a leotard created by British designer Vivienne Westwood (1984) from the collection of the V&A Museum.

Serghei Starus

A repeated multicoloured, square pattern in wool cloth created from the coloured threads used to weave it. Designs are associated with Scottish clans and have setts or pattern sizes that vary according to the weight of the cloth and the mill that produces it. In general, the heavier the weight the larger the sett. The broader colour bands are the under check, which may be adorned with narrower colour lines called the over check. Most tartans use the three-colour design for the Black Watch regiment, which at one time was the only legal pattern.

☞ see Balfour 30, Kilt 145, Punk 201

Royal Stewart

Angus

Bruce

Cameron

Black Watch

Gordon Regimental

Dermal pigmentation made by inserting coloured ink into the skin. Tattooing has been practised for centuries by many cultures across the world, from Japan to South America. The word may derive from the Samoan, Tongan or Tahitian *ta-tau* meaning to mark or strike twice and was first used in English by Captain James Cook in 1769. Tattooing was historically practised to denote status or rank, as part of ceremonies or for religious reasons, in addition to a means of identifying prisoners and slaves. Tattooing in the Western world is primarily used for permanent cosmetic reasons.

MaxFX

☞ see Punk 201

A dress or gown that extends to the end of the shin. Examples of tea length hemlines can be found on women's day gowns from the late 19th to mid-20th centuries, with unstructured lines, light fabrics and feminine detailing.

Zoe Irvin

see Dress 95, Skirt Length 222

A repeated geometric design that covers a fabric without gaps or overlaps. Tessellation is used in fashion to provide a seamless pattern to present a constant and cohesive image. Pictured is a design that can cover a wide area by tessellation.

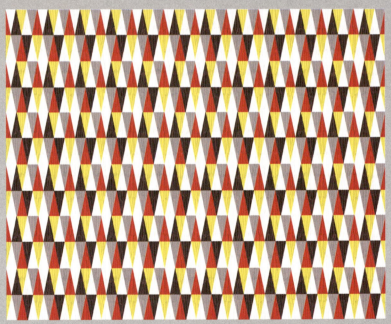

☞ see Pattern (fabric) 182, Print 198, Repeat 204

A concept or narrative maintained throughout a collection of clothes that imbibes them with a certain attitude or viewpoint. A clothing collection can be themed in many ways such as nautical, African or twisted, as in the examples pictured here for jeans manufacturer Levi's. The garments in this collection are twisted as part of their construction, which is reflected in the images contained in this promotional brochure or look book.

see Collection 71, Concept 74, Look Book 155

A narrow piece of cloth that passes between the buttocks to cover the genitals and attaches to a band around the hips. The first thongs are believed to have been worn 75,000 years ago in Africa. Thongs (also known as g-strings, though these tend to use less material) have become a popular female underwear garment as they do not produce a visible panty line. Both men and women wear thong swimsuits. Thongs can also describe sandals that are attached to the wearer's foot by a thong positioned inside the big toe.

☞ see Lingerie 153

Niaam Wind

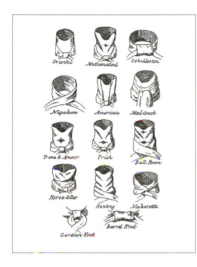

Dimple

A piece of cloth that is tied with a knot at the throat and worn under a shirt collar. The tie developed from cravats, tied with a bow knot and introduced as part of formal court wear by Charles II of England in the 15th century. Tie etiquette dictates that the thick end should be level with the trouser waist and the thin end should never drop below the thick end.

Four in hand or simple knot

A tying method that produces a narrow, discreet and slightly asymmetrical tie knot with a dimple for use with a standard button-down dress shirt. Popular in Britain since the 1850s and perhaps named after a London gentleman's club, it is the simplest knot to tie.

Half Windsor

A simplified variant of the Windsor knot that gives a neat, triangular knot.

Windsor, full Windsor or double Windsor

A tying method that produces a wide triangular knot with two dimples at the side, named after the Duke of Windsor.

Pratt or Shelby knot

A symmetrical knot that begins with the tie's reverse side facing out, created by Jerry Pratt, but popularised by TV personality Don Shelby. It is suitable for shorter ties as it uses less length than a half Windsor or Windsor.

A garment created as a test for a new pattern of design, typically from cheap material such as gingham cloth or calico. A toile or muslin allows the designer to see how a design works and hangs, allowing it to be altered and perfected prior to producing the finished garment.

☞ **see Fabric 107**

Toile de Jouy or toile is a decorative pattern with a repeated scene in black or dark colour against a white background. Toile de Jouy means cloth from Jouy-en-Josas in north-central France (*teile* meaning cloth).

see Pattern (fabric) 182

A tall, flat-crowned, broad-brimmed hat first made by John Hetherington in 1797 and worn by men throughout the 19th century for business and social events. Made from stiffened beaver fur felt or silk, the top hat or 'topper', declined in popularity towards the end of the century, but was retained for formal occasions by the upper class and continues to be used for formal wear such as with a morning suit and evening dress.

☞ **see Hats 128**

A sewing technique used for item edges that gives a crisp edge and helps facings (fabric sewn over the base fabric) stay in place. Topstitching may use a thread that matches the colour of the fabric or use a contrasting colour, such as the orange thread used for denim jeans and jackets. Topstitch may also be used to form decorative designs in different coloured thread. Pictured is a piece of leather that has been topstitched for decorative purposes.

☞ see Stitches 225

prism_68

The long, rear part of a skirt or dress that trails behind the wearer. A train is often a separate garment called a court or bridal train and is worn with a court or wedding dress. The court train is based on the coloured tail plumage or train of a male peacock, a bird found in the menageries and grounds of many European royal houses.

see Bridal 55

A double-breasted, loose belted knee-length raincoat made of waterproof heavy-duty cotton drill or poplin, created by Thomas Burberry. Unlike a macintosh, which has rubberised fabric, a trench coat achieves waterproofing through the closely woven twill construction. Water droplets rest on the surface and run off.

see Coat 68, Macintosh 156

A period in English history (1485–1603) when the Tudor dynasty held the English throne. Fashions in this period migrated from low-slung necks and ample sleeves (such as those pictured in this image by Hans Holbein) to a more formal look with large neck ruffs in the late Elizabethan age. For women, tight corsets and full, triangular dresses changed so that bodices were longer and skirts more circular. Petticoats, chemises, stockings and corsets were all popular.

☞ see Elizabethan 101, Neck 176, Ruff 209

Vera Bogaerts

A headdress made from a long, single piece of cloth wound round the head or inner hat, particularly by Sikh and Muslim men. Muslim turban colour may indicate status as a black turban is a claim to status as a descendant of Muhammad, while a white turban in Sudan indicates high social status. Sikh turbans, on the other hand, generally have no such connotation with turbans coloured to coordinate with outfits, although orange and navy turbans are traditionally worn on religious days.

Billy Lobo H.

A wrap-around skirt with attaching bodice worn by ballet dancers. Tutu skirts may be a single hanging layer or be made up of multiple starched layers that strut out in order to show off the ballerina's footwork. The classic short tutu is made with layers of stiff netting with a slight bell shape and is featured in paintings by French Impressionist artist Edgar Degas (pictured below left is *The Dance Class*). Tutu is a corruption of the French *cucu*, baby talk for *cul*, meaning buttocks.

Manuel Velasco

Formal wear comprising a black, ventless dinner or smoking jacket with silk or satin lapels. The tuxedo is typically worn with a white shirt, black tie and cummerbund. It was developed in the early 19th century, following on from the white tie and tailcoat, and black bow tie and short mess jacket of military origin (made popular by the Prince of Wales in 1865). The term originates from the Tuxedo Club in New York, where the dinner jacket was first used in the USA. French designer Yves Saint Laurent created the 'Le Smoking' female version in 1966.

☞ see Cummerbund 83, Eveningwear 106, Tie 243

A matching cardigan and jumper set worn by women. The twin set sweater is typically tight fitting, has short sleeves and a round neck over which the cardigan is worn unbuttoned, often with pearls. Twin sets first appeared in the 1940s.

Zoe Irvin

A fabric that is used underneath the face fabric in the construction of a garment. Underlining fabrics such as light- to medium-weight cotton batiste or silk organza are cut from the same pattern pieces as the top fabric and are attached before garment construction begins, and subsequently handled as a single item with the fashion or face fabric. Underlining adds stability and strength to lightweight fabrics, and reduces wrinkling and transparency.

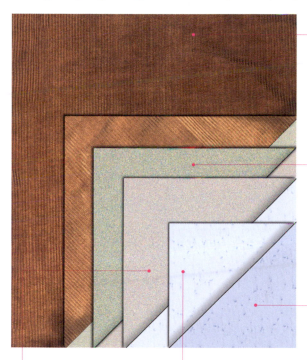

Face fabric/garment fabric
The visible outer fabric of the garment.

Underlining
Applied before interfacing, interlining and lining, underlining prevents stretching, adds support and opacity.

Lining
A slippery fabric attached at a garment's waistband, neck or hem to give a finished look inside the garment. Prevents seams unravelling and helps it slide on and off.

Interfacing
A layer between underlining and interlining to help support and shape a garment and stabilise its edges.

Interlining
A layer applied before the lining to provide warmth.

A set of identical clothes worn by members of an organisation or group. Uniforms are worn in many institutions – from schools, companies, retail outlets, sports and other clubs – to the military, police, fire and other services. Uniform dressing is also found in everyday common usage as people wear clothes to identify with social groupings or preferences and as a sense of identity.

Anthony Fournier

Clothing that primarily serves a functional purpose, such as providing warmth, protection or some other practical use. The majority of work clothes that one associates to a particular profession are utilitarian, but such garments are sometimes adopted into mainstream fashion. Denim jeans were originally hard-wearing work trousers developed for Californian gold miners. Contemporary designers have appropriated utilitarian values and styles as can be seen through the various interpretations of the cargo pant: a loose-fitting trouser with several deep pockets and a hammer loop, traditionally worn by skilled manual workers such as carpenters. The emphasis in such a garment is on practicality rather than style although, through appropriation, it often becomes a style.

☞ see Denim 90, Uniform 256

Alexandra Gleitz

A fabric produced with different coloured yarns or threads to provide streaks, marks, or patches of different colours. Knitting can produce a complex variegated pattern by both using yarn that contains streaks, and combining different yarns in the knit, as pictured. By manipulation of the warp and weft, flowers and a variegated colour can appear in the weave of brocade.

► see Brocade 56, Knitting 148, Weave 265

An opening in the fabric that allows for greater movement. Vents are typically seen rising vertically from the bottom hem of jackets to extend over the hips so as to prevent the garment being too tight.

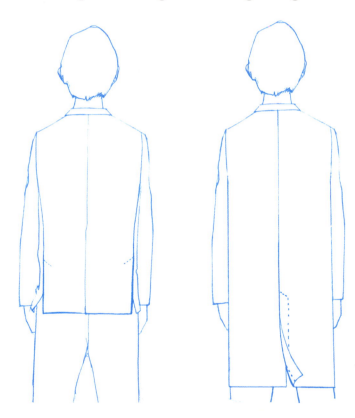

☞ see Darts 87, Jacket 140, Suit 229

Garments and accessories from the Victorian period (1837–1901) or that reflect the tastes of the time. Fashion Victoriana includes tailcoats and top hats for men, and floor-length, hooped silk dresses trimmed with frills, flounces, lace, braid and ribbons for women.

☞ see Basque 33, Corsage 76, Corset 77, Ribbon 207, Top Hat 246

The Dover Press

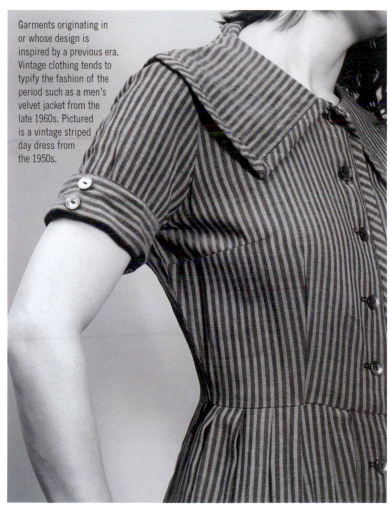

Garments originating in or whose design is inspired by a previous era. Vintage clothing tends to typify the fashion of the period such as a men's velvet jacket from the late 1960s. Pictured is a vintage striped day dress from the 1950s.

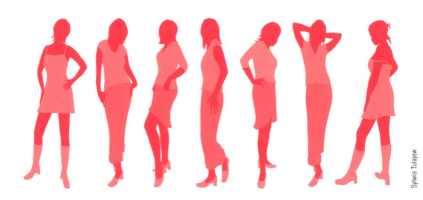

Sylwia Tulajew

The current fashion or trend. What is 'in vogue' changes frequently and for any number of reasons. These often include the changing styles of fashion leaders such as pop stars, film stars and footballers. Taste tends to fluctuate over time, seeing things such as hemlines, hair length and trouser tightness constantly evolving. For example, from the 1920s shorter skirts were in vogue, a trend that peaked in the 1960s with the miniskirt. This was followed by a fad for the micro-skirt, before skirt lengths became longer again in the 1970s. Each generation of designers tends, to some extent, to recycle fashion elements from a previous era. A fad is a fashion that is popular for a brief moment in time, while a trend is something that develops over a longer period of time.

A sleeveless, upper-body garment cut at waist level with a vertical, button-fastened front opening worn over a dress shirt and underneath a suit jacket of a three-piece suit. Called a vest in the USA and Canada, a waistcoat was worn with braces or suspenders rather than a belt, and featured a pocket for a pocket watch before the wristwatch was invented.

see Button 60, Jacket 140, Suit 229

Interlinking threads or yarns that are woven to make cloth on a loom. The warp is the lengthwise yarn through which the horizontal weft yarn is shuttled back and forth. Warp means that which is thrown across, from the German *weorpan*, meaning to throw. The weft can be shuttled across the warp in different ways to make different patterns in the cloth.

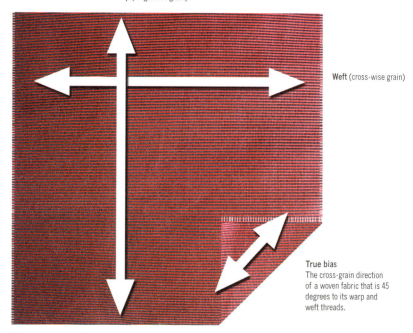

Warp (lengthwise grain)

Weft (cross-wise grain)

True bias
The cross-grain direction of a woven fabric that is 45 degrees to its warp and weft threads.

Selvage
The uncut fabric edge as it comes off the loom.

☞ see Bias 36, Selvage 214

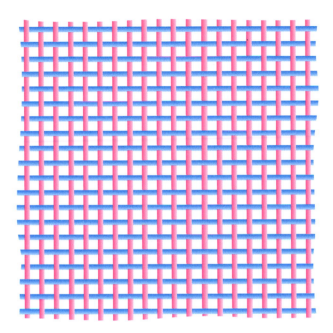

The pattern of interlinking threads or yarns called the warp and weft created during the cloth production process on a loom. Different weaves produce different texture and visual elements to the cloth, with the main weaves being plain, twill and satin. Plain weave is used to produce calico, chiffon and flannel; twill weave is used for denim, drill and tweed; and satin weave for a smooth finish. The cloth can also be coloured or patterned by using different coloured warp and weft.

☞ see Knitting 148, Warp & Weft 264

A horizontal stitch for joining two pieces of fabric, giving a ribbing appearance, such as the seam of a baseball. Welt stitch also refers to the trim ribbing at the hem, cuffs and neck of a knitted garment. Welt stitching can also be used to attach the sole of a shoe to the upper.

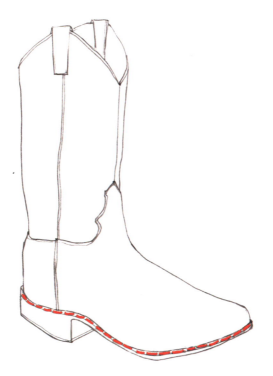

Anthony Fourrier

☞ see Stitches 225

A fibre found in the coats of sheep and other animals of the caprinae family, such as sheep, goats, alpacas and rabbits. Wool is different to fur in that it has overlapping scales and is crimped, thus making it easier to spin (as the fibres easily attach to each other). The crimp increases textile bulk and allows it to retain air and therefore heat. Wool quality is determined by fibre fineness, length, scale structure, colour, cleanliness and freedom from damage, and is graded according to its diameter in microns. Fine wool is softer, whereas wool with a diameter of up to 25 microns is much coarser and is used for outerwear. This coarser wool is named 'merino' after the sheep breed that it comes from. Wool quality is indicated in the UK through use of the Woolmark and Woolmark Blend symbols pictured.

< 17.5 Ultrafine merino   17.6–18.5 Superfine merino
< 19.5 Fine merino   19.6–20.5 Fine medium merino

☞ **see Alpaca 20, Mohair 172**

Charles Frederick Worth is regularly credited as being the father of haute couture. He dominated Parisian fashion during the 19th century and was the first designer to display garments on live models at the House of Worth. His creations were shown at the Great Exhibition in London in 1851 and the Exposition Universelle in Paris in 1855 (pictured above). Pictured right are chiffon evening dresses created with sequins, satin and embroidery by House of Worth in 1928–29.

V&A Images/Victoria and Albert Museum

☞ **see Haute Couture 129, Model 171, Tailoring 232**

Any long, continuous piece of entwined fibre that is used for the production of textiles or knits. Yarn is used to make fabric while thread is used to sew different fabrics together. Yarn can be produced from a range of natural and synthetic fibres such as cotton, wool, flax, alpaca, angora, cashmere, silk, nylon and polyester and can be dyed to produce fabrics with a wide range of colours.

Yarn production accelerated during the Industrial Revolution due to the demand from mechanised textile mills in England and other countries. Pictured is dyed wool yarn, hanging prior to weaving.

David Kay

☞ see Alpaca 20, Industrial Revolution 137

A fabric cut that is seamed across the top of a shirt, trouser or skirt. Quality shirts typically have a two-piece split yoke to ensure an excellent fit across the shoulders. A yoke is also a decorative fabric attached to the top of a garment around the neck and over the shoulders.

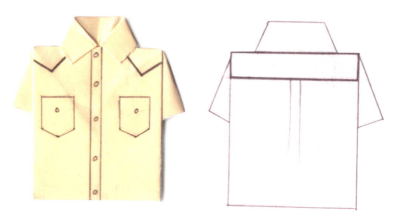

Anthony Fourrier

☞ see Neck 176

V&A Images/Victoria and Albert Museum

The moral and intellectual trends of a given era. Taken from the German *zeit* meaning time and *geist* meaning spirit, the term's literal translation is 'the spirit of the age'. Fashion, art and design are all subject to the zeitgeist and this is reflected in everything from choice of colours, hemlines, hairstyles and cosmetics. As such, certain designs can be easily classified as originating in a certain era. Pictured is a conceptual chic evening dress created by Zandra Rhodes, together with a bondage suit created by Vivienne Westwood (1977), reflecting the punk zeitgeist of the late 1970s.

The Details

1600s
The First Suits
Block-printed calico first exported from India to England in 1630. Cravats, the predecessor to the modern tie, entered Parisian culture. Trousers and jackets for men were cut from the same material, an early form of what we know today as the suit.

1750–1850
The Industrial Revolution
The Industrial Revolution saw independently powered machines replace the spinning wheel and hand loom, while improvements in raw material production ignited the growth of the weaving industry, dominated by manufactured cotton from England. Pictured is Manchester, nicknamed 'Cottonopolis'.

1750–1850
The Cotton Trade
Cotton goods were exported around the world as the Industrial Revolution in Britain allowed mass manufacture following the invention of the spinning jenny in 1764. Cotton has remained a staple commodity in world fibre trade and is a mainstay of the textile industry.

Fashionable Evening Dress for September

1795–1820
Empire Influences
The Regency period during which the empire look was popular for women's clothing. Dresses fitted close to the torso under the bust and fell loosely with soft, flowing skirts. Men wore jackets with high waist seams, high collars and breeches and boots.

1800s
Colonial Influences
The British occupation of India saw a cultural interchange that brought many styles and customs into British and European life, including these tight-fitting riding trousers that were named after the city of Jodhpur in India where they were originally worn.

1800s
The Birth of Mail Order
Mail order purchasing, whereby consumers select items from a catalogue and send, pay for and receive their order by mail, became popular in the 19th century with the development of the postal system. Mail order continues to be an important distribution channel for fashion retailers by allowing them to access consumers in remote locations in addition to those that prefer to shop from home.

1820s–1830s
The Creation of Elastic
Thomas Hancock patented elastic, which he used in a range of fastenings for gloves, suspenders, shoes and stockings.

1823
The Discovery of Waterproof Fabric
In 1823 Scottish chemist Charles Macintosh created a waterproof raincoat using a fabric he invented.

1834–1896
The Arts and Crafts Movement
English artist, writer, socialist and activist William Morris was a founder of the British Arts and Crafts Movement, and is well known for his wallpaper and fabric designs. Morris sought to reverse the demise of beauty at the hands of the Industrial Revolution, and re-establish the link between the worker and art through an honesty in design.

1837–1901
Victorian Fashions
The Victorian age saw widespread use of tailcoats and top hats for men and floor-length, hooped silk dresses trimmed with frills, flounces, lace, braid and ribbons for women.

1850s–1860s
Charles Frederick Worth
Englishman Charles Frederick Worth opened the first haute couture fashion house in Paris in 1858. The dinner jacket or tuxedo became popular formal wear in 1865 after it was worn by the Prince of Wales.

1853
The Birth of Denim
Levi Strauss began a wholesale business to provide denim clothing to Californian Gold Rush miners. Levi Strauss & Co. has popularised denim to such an extent that it has now become a staple for leisurewear.

1901–1910
Edwardian Fashions

The *Belle Epoque* period saw fashions become more cosmopolitan under the influence of international travel and art nouveau. Sports clothing also developed for the leisure class. Paul Poiret, the creator of harem pants and the first couturier to launch a perfume, called Rosina, established his fashion house in 1906.

1913
Coco Chanel

Modernist French fashion designer Gabrielle Bonheur Coco Chanel (1883–1971) opened a boutique in Deauville, France. Chanel went on to revolutionise women's fashion with the Chanel suit, chain-belted jerseys and sunglasses with elegant simplicity. Chanel popularised the little black dress and started the trend for suntans, having got burnt on a 1923 cruise.

1914–1918
The First World War

The First World War saw women adopt men's clothing as they went to work in factories. The military influence on fashion grew with garments such as the trenchcoat created by Thomas Burberry, made of a waterproof heavy-duty cotton drill or poplin. Burberry also invented gabardine and the red, white, black, and peach Nova check that became known as his trademark Burberry check.

c.1920
The Flapper Style

New styles developed in the 'roaring twenties' to cater for flappers; young women who wore bobbed hair, short skirts and make-up, listened to jazz and partied hard. The flapper style accentuated a thin, elongated boyish shape with straight and loose dresses. Underwear developed to cater for this new lifestyle with bras that flattened the bust and step-in knickers.

1920s
Fashionable Fragrance

The decade that saw the rise of French designer Coco Chanel. In 1921, Chanel No.5 perfume, the first perfume to be sold worldwide, was launched. Later in the decade Chanel created the LBD or little black dress, a variation on the cocktail dress.

1926
The Rise and Fall of Hemlines

Hemlines began rising after 1910 and soon raced up the leg to become near knee-length by 1926, in order to be compatible with the Charleston dancing style. Rayon, or artificial silk, became increasingly popular and caused a decline in cotton use. In 1926, Waldo Semon found a way to plasticise PVC, making it commercially viable.

1930s
The Appearance of Logos
French tennis star Rene Lacoste – *La Crocodile* – launched a loose-knit short sleeved pique cotton tennis shirt with embroidered crocodile, perhaps the first designer logo to appear on clothing. The Lacoste apparel company was founded in 1933. Nylon was developed, but widespread use did not occur until the 1940s. In this decade the houndstooth check appeared, and although invented in the 1800s, the fashion mannequin became widely popular.

1940s
The Launch of the Bikini
The bikini, a two-piece swimsuit, was launched in 1946 and became a fixture of women's wardrobes, progressively shrinking to the thong in the 1980s. Capri pants were created by Italian designer Emilio Pucci in 1949. The twin set, a matching cardigan and jumper worn by women, appeared. French designer Christian Dior re-established Paris as a fashion centre in 1947 through his 'new look', which revived haute couture and feminine beauty following wartime austerity.

1950s
Rockabilly Style
The rockabilly style of denim jeans and jacket became popular through its use by the singer Elvis Presley. This developed into the greaser look, characterised by long sideburns, greased back hair, tight jeans or black slacks, brothel creeper shoes, motorcycle jackets and tattoos. Stiletto heeled shoes were launched after a 1952 Christian Dior show.

1958
Mary Quant

Designer Mary Quant began experimenting with shorter skirts at her London boutique Bazaar in the late 1950s and was credited with inventing the miniskirt, one of the fashions that defined the 1960s. Quant considered a skirt with a hemline well above the knees to be liberating.

Late 1950s–1960s
Mods and Rockers

The British mod subculture developed around fashion and music and was characterised by slim-cut Italian suits, modern jazz and rhythm and blues. Mods developed a unique style based around continental clothes, scooters, French new wave cinema and existentialist philosophy. The movement adopted the RAF circumpunct symbol of concentric circles. Mods often clashed with rockers, a later variation of the rockabillies and teddy boys of the 1940s and 1950s.

1960s
Baby Doll Dresses as Outerwear

Although launched as outerwear in 1957/58, baby doll dresses became one of the iconic fashion statements of the 1960s and 1970s.

1960s
Deconstruction in Fashion

French philosopher Jacques Derrida used the term 'deconstruction' to describe a method of critical enquiry examining how meaning is constructed by challenging the prescribed values that are presented to us. The fashion industry has used deconstruction principles to create clothes that do not conform to traditional garment conceptions by being taken apart and put back together, unfinished, inside out or in some other way deteriorated.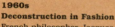

Early 1960s
The Creation of the First Ready-to-Wear Collection

Italian-born French designer Pierre Cardin was the first designer to license his name for different products. Known for an avant-garde style and designs using geometric shapes and motifs, Cardin frequently ignored the female form in favour of a unisex approach. Cardin launched the first ready-to-wear collection in 1959 for the Printemps department store in Paris.

1962
The Launch of Yves Saint Laurent

After working with Christian Dior, French designer Yves Saint Laurent opened his own fashion house using his YSL initials as its brand. The house led fashion trends such as the beatnik look, tweed suits, tight pants and tall, thigh-high boots.

Mid-1960s
Futuristic Fashions and an Acceptance of Nudity

Influenced by the modernist or mod music scene, London became the centre of the fashion world with fun, colourful clothes, gaining widespread appeal through the use of psychedelic prints and wild colours made in materials from vinyl to paper. Austrian designer Rudi Gernreich pushed the boundaries of a futuristic look with creations such as the 1964 topless swimsuit (or monokini) and the bra-less, see-through blouse look. The micro-skirt follows the miniskirt and takes hemlines to a new height.

1968
The Launch of America's Biggest Names

Two of the biggest names in fashion got their start as American designers; Calvin Klein and Ralph Lauren began production in New York. Calvin Klein's designs featured elegant, simple forms presented in neutral earth tones and luxurious fabrics. Ralph Lauren (pictured) started with menswear, but expanded into womenswear, again favouring natural fabrics, but with western and country motifs that were subsequently sold under the Polo brand.

1968
Unisex

The term 'unisex' was first used to descibe clothes that were produced or adjusted to be worn by either gender.

1970
Glam Trends
American designer Roy Halston Frowick dominated female fashion with pantsuit creations, sweater sets and form-fitting dresses in earth tones. Halston licensed his designs and JC Penney made his designs accessible to women at various income levels. Popularised by glam rock music, platform boots saw people add a few inches to their height. Together with flared or bell-bottom trousers, platform boots have been one of the enduring and defining fashion items of the decade.

1970s
The Punk Subculture
The punk subculture developed around the punk rock music scene in London and New York. Punk fashion was commercialised by Vivienne Westwood and Malcolm McLaren through their London boutique SEX, a deconstructionist, anti-fashion establishment designed to be confrontational, rebellious and shocking with a disdain for established norms and niceties.

Early 1980s
Japanese Influences
The Japanese school rose to prominence as designers such as Issey Miyake, Kenzo Takada, Rei Kawakubo and Hanae Mori enjoyed increasing success in the world of couture. The goth subculture emerged with a clothing style characterised by dyed black hair, black eyeliner and nail polish, ear, facial and body piercings, and black clothes, often drawing on Victorian dress influences.

1984
Fashion as a Political Statement
Slogans on t-shirts were appropriated by the fashion industry after designer Katherine Hamnett met UK Prime Minister Margaret Thatcher while wearing an anti-nuclear t-shirt.

1990s
The Rise of Alexander McQueen
'Anything goes' became the motto as designers such as English designer Alexander McQueen produced shocking designs that featured cozy, romantic garments, dresses that looked like quilt blankets and rabbit-skin garments. Following his appointment as head designer at Givenchy in 1996, McQueen continued indulging his rebellious streak with double amputee model Aimee Mullins striding down the catwalk on intricately carved wooden legs.

1999–present
The Growth of E-shopping
Shopping online via the Internet saw the application of computer technology to the mail order concept. Consumers can now select products from an on-line electronic catalogue and place and pay for their orders via computer, with the merchandise delivered by mail within days.

This book aims to enhance the understanding and appreciation of fashion design by providing a reference to the many terms used within the discipline, in addition to providing an insight into some of the historic and cultural aspects that have helped shape its development. Fashion design is a vibrant and progressive pursuit that seeks to incorporate new ideas from all parts of society. We hope that this book helps you better understand and further your own ideas.

The difference between cocktail dresses and evening wear is discussed on pages 69 and 106 respectively.

Zoe Irvin

Acknowledgements

We would like to thank everyone who supported us during the production of this book including the many art directors, designers and creatives who showed great generosity in allowing us to reproduce their work. Special thanks to everyone that hunted for, collated, compiled and rediscovered some of the work examples contained in this book. Thanks also to Zoe Irvin and Anthony Fourrier for their fantastic and inpirational illustration work, and to Rachel Lloyd at the V&A for all her help and support. Also, a big thank you to Brett Phillips at 3 Deep Design, Jeff Knowles at Research Studios, Parent Design and Studio Thomson for their support and help. A final thank you is due to Caroline Walmsley and Leafy Robinson at AVA Publishing who never tired of our requests, enquiries and questions, and supported us throughout.

Whilst this volume is by no means exhaustive, we have tried our best to include all those terms that are most commonly used in the realm of fashion design. If you feel that we have missed any entries then please do let us know by sending an email, marked Visual Dictionary Entries, to enquiries@avabooks.co.uk. Please include your name and address and if your entry makes it to an updated, later edition of the book then we'll send you a copy for free!

Additional image credits: p.7: Zoe Irvin / p.8, far right: The Dover Press / p.9: Anthony Fourrier / p.10, below: The Dover Press / p.11, left: The Dover Press, right: Zoe Irvin / p.28: Ben Heys / p.30: The Dover Press / p.37: Imacon / p.61: Sandra Caldwell / p.104: Duncan Walker / p.121: 7382489561 / p.132: Michael Westhoff / p.143: Duncan Walker / p.145: Louis Aguinaldo (istockphoto) / p.150: stocksnapper / p.151: Beth Van Trees / p.153: Morgan Lane Photography / p.155: Parent Design / p.157: Xavier Young / p.177, bottom left: The Dover Press / p.183: The Dover Press / p.189: The Dover Press / p.212: Andrew Perris / p.237: The Dover Press / p.241 Rob Petrie / p.243 Tie / p.244 Andrew Perris / p.247 Yury Zaporozhchenko